CAMBRIDGE
Global English

for Cambridge Primary English as a Second Language

Learner's Book 1

Elly Schottman & Caroline Linse

Series Editor: Kathryn Harper

Contents

Page	Unit	Words and expressions	Use of English	Reading/Writing
10–17	Starter	Greetings Parts of the body Colours Actions Objects Letters of the alphabet	Numbers 1–10	Read/Recite a poem Write name, numbers and colour words
18–33	1 Welcome to school	School objects and activities Greetings and introductions Colours Vehicles Feelings Things in nature	Singular and plural nouns Proper nouns Present simple Subject pronouns: *I, you, we, he, she* Possessive adjectives: *my, your, his, her*	Word labels, poems, songs, charts Read for information Picture walk **Guided writing:** Poem, information about self
34–49	2 Family time	Family members Home and school activities Food: likes and dislikes Numbers 0–10 Days of the week	Singular and plural nouns; proper nouns Numbers: 0–10 Present simple: statements, questions, short answers Prepositions of location: *in, at* Use *with* and *for*	Poems, songs Read for information Environmental print **Guided writing:** Cards, information about self, recipe
50–65	3 Fun and games	Actions, sports, games Parts of the body Language of good sportsmanship Point to/put Animals Feelings	*can/can't* for ability Numbers: 1–12 Prepositions of location: *on, under, next to* Possessive adjectives Present simple	Poem, story, play Read for information Text features (identify characters in a play script) **Guided writing:** Simple words spelled aloud, information about self, new song verse, story sequel
66–67	Check your progress 1			
68–83	4 Making things	Clothes Shapes Art activities Colours and other descriptive adjectives	Present continuous: statements and questions Subject pronouns Contractions: *I'm, she's, they're*, etc. Connective: *and* Numbers: 1–20 Use *for* Use *like* + verb + *–ing*	Poem, song, traditional folktale Read for information Understand words through context Set a purpose for reading **Guided writing:** Information about self, new song verse, thank you note

Contents

Listening/Speaking	Cross-curricular links	Phonics/Word study	21st-century skills
Greet friends Ask and answer questions Understand and repeat conversations Sing and act out TPR songs	**Science:** Colour-mixing experiments **Maths:** Count 1–10, measure (non-standard units)	Alphabet song and chant	Make new friends Play, work and learn together **Critical thinking:** Do experiments Record results
Listen for details Understand words through context Follow TPR directions Ask and answer questions Spell own name Interview and introduce a friend Play a guessing game Sing a spelling song Act out a poem	**Global awareness** (Social studies): School children around the world **Maths:** Understand and enter information on a chart	Letter names Alphabet poem	Activate prior knowledge Work collaboratively Share ideas, information **Critical thinking:** Discuss and enter data on a chart Compare and contrast Predict story events Reflection/self-assessment **Values:** Appreciating the world around us
Listen for main idea and details Ask and answer questions Participate in conversations Play a counting game, sing a counting song Say, sing, act out poems and songs	**Maths:** 0–10 Simple problem-solving Record and discuss information on charts	Read and write words with short *a* Consonant digraph: *th* Rhyming words	Activate prior knowledge Work collaboratively **Critical thinking:** Classify Conduct a survey Create and discuss charts Reflection/Self-assessment **Values:** We love our families
Follow and give instructions Understand words through context Listen for details and main idea Recognise simple words spelled aloud Play games Ask and answer questions	**Global awareness** (Social studies): Games from different places **Maths:** Count 1–12 Problem-solving Use charts	Read and write words with short *u* Read and write short *a* words (revise) Read and act out a phonics story	Activate prior knowledge Work collaboratively Share ideas, information **Critical thinking:** Creative problem-solving Compare and contrast Sequence Reflection/Self-assessment **Values:** Recognise feelings, show empathy
Listen for main idea and details Ask and answer questions Describe what people are wearing and doing Describe pictures Say, sing and act out poems, songs, stories	**Maths:** Count 1–20 Identify simple geometric shapes **Art:** Make puppets	Read and write words with a short *e* Identify rhyming words Read a phonics story	Express creativity through art Share ideas, information **Critical thinking:** Classify Draw conclusions Reflection/Self-assessment **Values:** Saying thank you

Contents

Page	Unit	Words and expressions	Use of English	Reading/Writing
84–99	5 On the farm	Farm animals and crops Farming activities Describe life cycle of animals and plants Parts of a plant Ongoing actions Polite language: asking for help	Present continuous (statements, questions, short answers) Adverbs of place: *here/there* *can/can't* for ability Contractions Prepositions of location: *in, above*	Poem, song, stories Read for information: life cycle diagrams Understand words through context Scan for main idea **Guided writing:** Simple words spelled aloud, word cards, life cycles, story ending
100–115	6 My five senses	Our five senses Parts of the body Musical instruments Adjectives to describe sight, sound, taste, touch Fruits	Present continuous Present simple: positive, negative statements, questions, short answers Descriptive adjectives Ordinals: 1st–3rd *can/can't* for ability Preposition of location: *on*	Poem, song, stories Read for information Making predictions **Guided writing:** Write about favourite sounds Write speech bubbles for a story
106–117	Check your progress 2			
118–133	7 Let's go!	Vehicles and parts of vehicles Ways to move Descriptions: size, colours, numbers Safety equipment: helmets, seatbelts	*can* + verb Simple present (positive and negative statements; questions) Adjective order *(big blue boat, two red sails)* *like* + verb + *–ing* Prepositions of location: *on, in, under, at, near*	Poem, songs, simple instructions Read for information Text features: headings **Guided writing:** Words spelled aloud Words on charts and diagram Sentences Information about self
134–149	8 City places	City sights and sounds City buildings and public places Ordinal numbers: 1st–10th Describe objects and people Opposites	Present simple *can/can't* + verb *like* + verb + *–ing* Prepositions of location: *in, on, next to, near* Demonstratives: *this/that* Pronouns: *this/these* Adverbs of place: *here, there* Connective: *and* Use *with* and *for*	Poems, song Read for information Understand words through context Scanning **Guided writing:** Sentences about city sights and sounds Sentences to express and explain a personal preference
150–165	9 Wonderful water	Water and living things Weather and clothing Nature Days of the week *Morning, afternoon, night* Daily routines	Present simple (positive/negative statements, questions, short answers) Contractions *Can/can't* + verb yes/no questions *Don't forget ...* Prepositions of time: *in, on, at*	Poems, song, story Read for information Read and act out a play Text type – folktale **Guided writing:** Words spelled aloud Sentences: initial capitalisation, full stop Connective: *and* Write dialogue in speech bubbles
166–167	Check your progress 3			
168–175	Picture dictionary	Review of vocabulary and themes		

4

Contents

Listening/Speaking	Cross-curricular links	Phonics/Word study	21st-century skills
Listen for main idea and details Recognise simple words spelled aloud Ask and answer questions Play guessing games Say, sing, act out poems, songs and stories Discuss opinions	**Science:** Life cycles (plants and animals) Living things Plant growth experiments; record observations	Read and write words with short *i* and other short vowels Consonant digraphs: *ch*, *sh* Rhyming words Tongue twisters Read a phonics story	Activate prior knowledge Work collaboratively Share ideas, information **Critical thinking:** Classify Sequence Discuss a story map Interpret and create diagrams Reflection/Self-assessment **Values:** Helping others
Listen for main idea and details Ask and answer questions Discuss favourite sounds and smells Identify objects by touch and by sound Describe objects using all the senses Express likes, dislikes Say, sing, act out poems, song, and stories	**Science:** Explore five senses with experiments and hands-on activities **Music:** Describe sounds Create musical sounds on home-made instruments	Read and write words with a short *i* and other short vowels Read a phonics story	Work collaboratively Share ideas, information **Critical thinking:** Compare and contrast Classify Identify opposites Enter information on charts Reflection/Self-assessment **Values:** Everyone is included
Listen for main idea and details Recognise simple words spelled aloud Follow and give instructions Ask and answer questions Describe objects Discuss preferences	**Science/Engineering:** Make a helicopter and a plane Experiment and record results	Read and write words with a long *e* – spelling *ee* Consonant digraph: *wh*	Integrate prior knowledge Work collaboratively Share ideas, information **Critical thinking:** Compare Classify Predict Enter and interpret information on charts Reflection/Self-assessment **Values:** Stay safe! Seatbelts, helmets and more
Listen for main idea and details Follow instructions Ask and answer questions Role-play; make requests Play a game Say and act out poems Express and explain opinions	**Global awareness:** (Social studies): City living **Maths:** Ordinals 1st–10th Identify and continue a repeating colour pattern	Clap and count syllables Sounds of final *–y* (long *e* or long *i*) Rhyming words	Activate prior knowledge Work collaboratively Share ideas, information **Critical thinking:** Opposites Compare and contrast Classify Sequence Reflection/Self-assessment **Values:** Appreciating where we live, respecting personal preference
Listen for details Ask and answer questions Participate in discussions Describe weather, objects and routine actions conversations Discuss and act out stories, poems, songs Link phrases with connective: *and*	**Science:** Water facts: Living things need water; water comes from rain and snow; animals that live in water Experiments with things that float: make predictions, do experiment, record results	Long *a* spellings *ai* and *ay* Read and act out a phonics story	Apply prior knowledge Work collaboratively Share ideas, information **Critical thinking:** Classify Research Predict outcomes Distinguish between read and make-believe Reflection/Self-assessment **Values:** Conserving water

5

How to use this book: **Learner**

How to use this book

In this book you will find lots of different features to help your learning.

What you will learn in the lesson. ⟶

> **We are going to...**
> - talk about things we can do.

Big questions to find out what you know already. ⟶

> **Getting started**
> What can we do for fun?
> Talk about what you know.
> Look at the picture for some ideas.

Important words and their meanings. These words are included on wordlists in the Teacher's Resource. ⟶

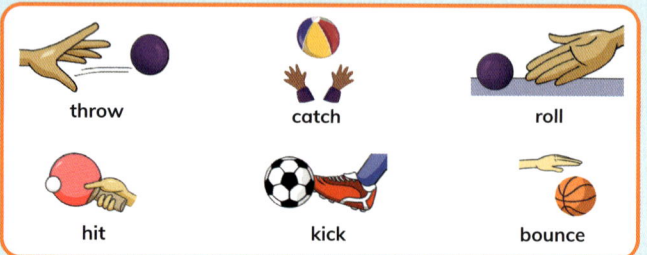

The key words include vocabulary from other subjects, instruction words and Academic English terms. ⟶

> **Key word**
> compare
>

Tips you can use to help you with your learning. ⟶

> **Reading tip**
> As you read, think about these questions:
> - How do the elves help the shoemaker?
> - How does the shoemaker help the elves?

Be a Language detective! Find out more about grammar. ⟶

> **Language detective**
>
> Where is her pencil?   Where is his pencil?
> Her pencil is _____ her nose.   His pencil is _____ his shoulder.

How to use this book

At the end of each unit, there is a choice of projects to work on together, using what you have learned. You might do some research or make something.

Questions help you think about how you learn.

Look at what you have learned in the unit! Think about which skills you do well and which you need more practice with.

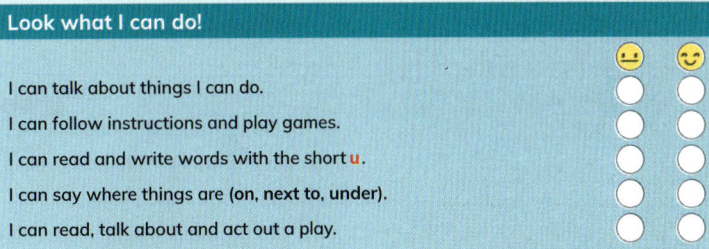

At the end of every 3 units, stop and check your progress! Play games and do activities to review what you have learned.

Use stickers to complete poems and to add to the Picture dictionary.

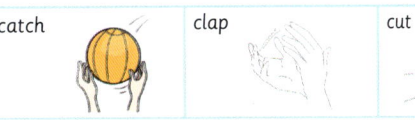

Audio is available with the Teacher's Resource or Digital Classroom

Video is available with Digital Classroom

How to use this book: Teacher

Lesson 1: The **Think About It** lesson introduces the topic through a big question and an image to generate discussion.

Many units include a video, available on Digital Classroom.

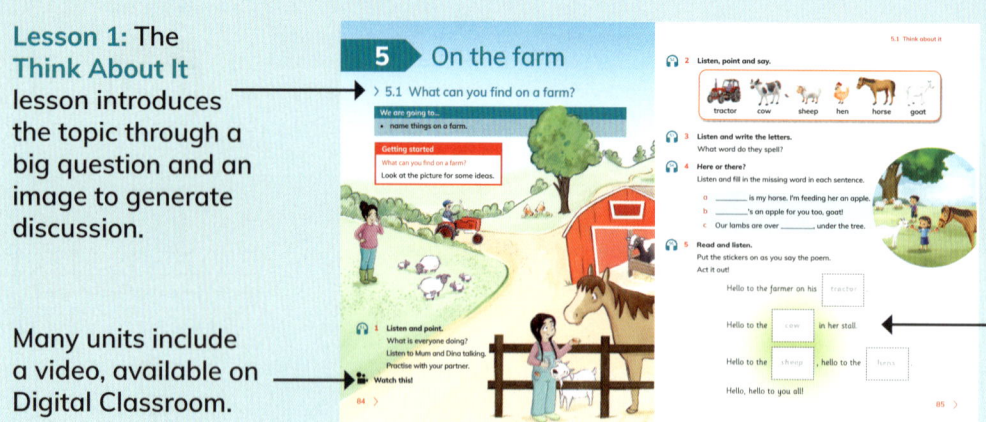

Poems include sticker activities to reinforce topic vocabulary.

Lesson 2: The **Let's Explore** lesson explores the unit topic further.

Lesson 3: The **cross-curricular** lesson prepares learners to learn in English across the curriculum.

In this lesson you'll find the key words.

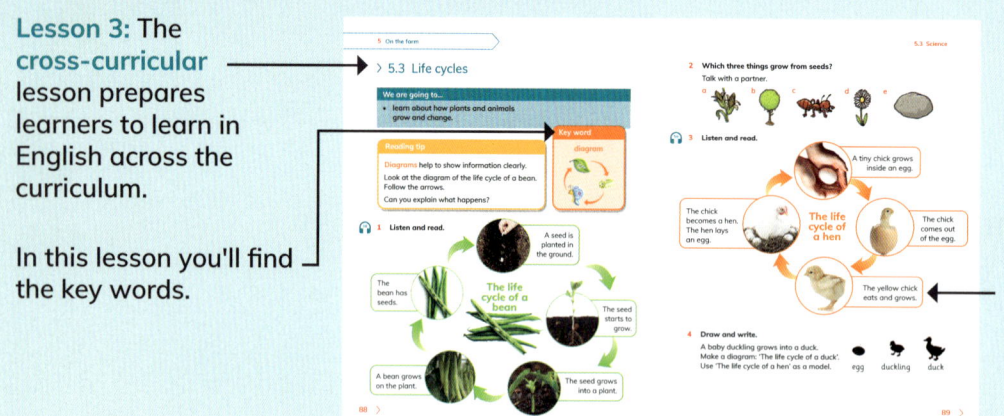

There are opportunities to think critically about the information in the text.

How to use this book

Lesson 4: The **Use of English** lesson develops grammar and includes a total physical response (TPR) song that practices some of the key language.

Language detective boxes present the main grammar point of each unit through an active learning approach. Digital Classroom includes grammar presentations.

Lesson 5: In Stage 1, the **Letters and Sounds** lesson develops phonics skills.

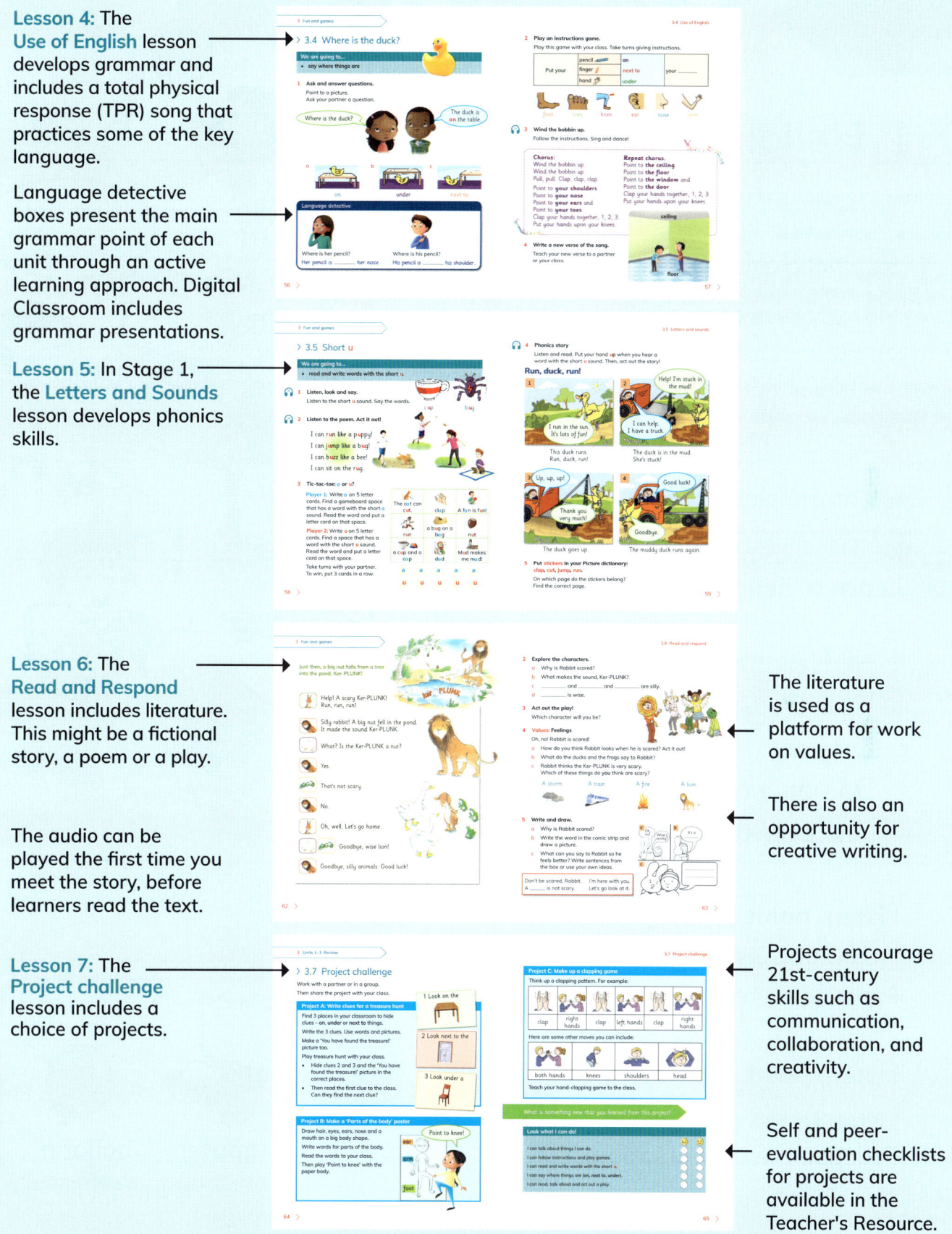

Lesson 6: The **Read and Respond** lesson includes literature. This might be a fictional story, a poem or a play.

The audio can be played the first time you meet the story, before learners read the text.

The literature is used as a platform for work on values.

There is also an opportunity for creative writing.

Lesson 7: The **Project challenge** lesson includes a choice of projects.

Projects encourage 21st-century skills such as communication, collaboration, and creativity.

Self and peer-evaluation checklists for projects are available in the Teacher's Resource.

Starter unit

> 1 Hello!

We are going to...
- say hello and make new friends
- name parts of the body.

Getting started

Talk about the things you know.
Look at the picture for more ideas.

 1 Learn a 'hello' poem.

> Hi! Hello! How are you?
> How are you today?
> I'm fine, thank you. How are you?
> Do you want to play?
> Yes! Let's play!

 2 Listen, point and say.

Listen to the boys talking.
Practise the conversation.

 3 Listen, point and say.

Listen to the girls talking.
Practise the conversation.

car   puppet   computer   balloon

1 Hello!

4 Head, shoulders, knees and toes

Listen to the song. Do the actions. Sing along!

head   shoulders   knees   toes

5 Play 'Simon Says!'

Listen carefully! If you hear 'Simon says, "Hop!"', do what Simon says.

If you hear 'Hop!', don't do it! Wait to hear 'Simon says, "Hop!"'

Starter unit

› 2 Colours

We are going to...
- talk about colours
- learn how to mix colours.

 1 **Sami has a blue hat.**
Listen and say.
Point to Sami, Meg and Liem.
Sing the song.

2 **Make a paper hat.**
You need:
- red, blue or green paper
- scissors
- paper clips or tape

What colour is your hat?

 3 **If you have a red hat...**
You will need your paper hats for this activity.
Listen to the song. Do the actions!

12

2 Science

4 Colour words

Point and say the colour words.

red yellow blue orange green purple

5 Mix blue and yellow.

Make handprints with paint.

Put a yellow   handprint on a blue  handprint.

What colour do you see?

6 Mix red and yellow.

Mix **red** modelling dough and **yellow** modelling dough together.

What colour do you see?

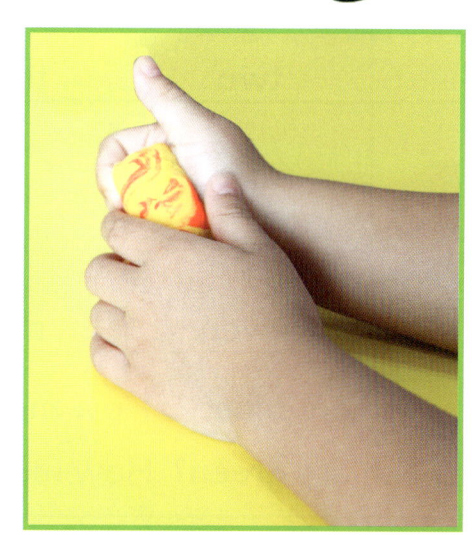

7 Mix red and blue.

Pour some **red** water and some **blue** water into a cup.

What colour do you see?

Starter unit

> 3 Numbers 1–10

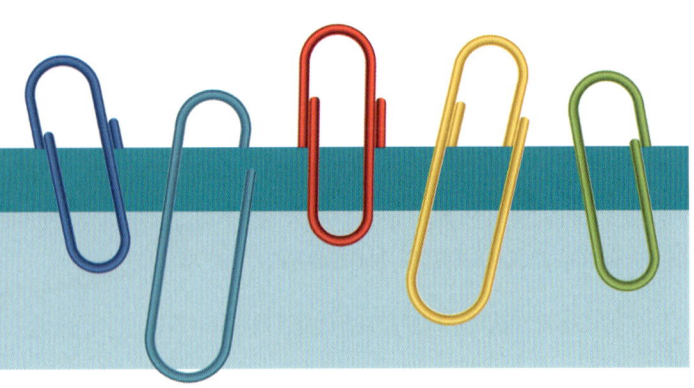

We are going to…
- count from 1 to 10
- use paper clips to measure.

1 Ten fish

Put a fish sticker in each box. Count the fish.

1 one	2 two	3 three	4 four	5 five
6 six	7 seven	8 eight	9 nine	10 ten

How many fish are **blue**?   How many fish are **yellow**?

How many fish are **green**?   How many fish have stripes?

 2 Sing a counting song.

One, two, three, four, five,
Once I caught a fish alive.
Six, seven, eight, nine, ten,
Then I threw it back again.

Why did you let it go?
Because it bit my finger so.
Which finger did it bite?
This little finger on my right.

3 Use of English

3 **How tall is the pencil?**

We can use paper clips to measure a pencil.

How tall is this pencil? _____ paper clips.

4 **Measure some more!**

Work with a partner.

Use paper clips  to measure.

Write the missing numbers.

a How tall are the scissors? _____ paper clips

b How tall is the ruler? _____ paper clips

c How tall is your book? _____ paper clips

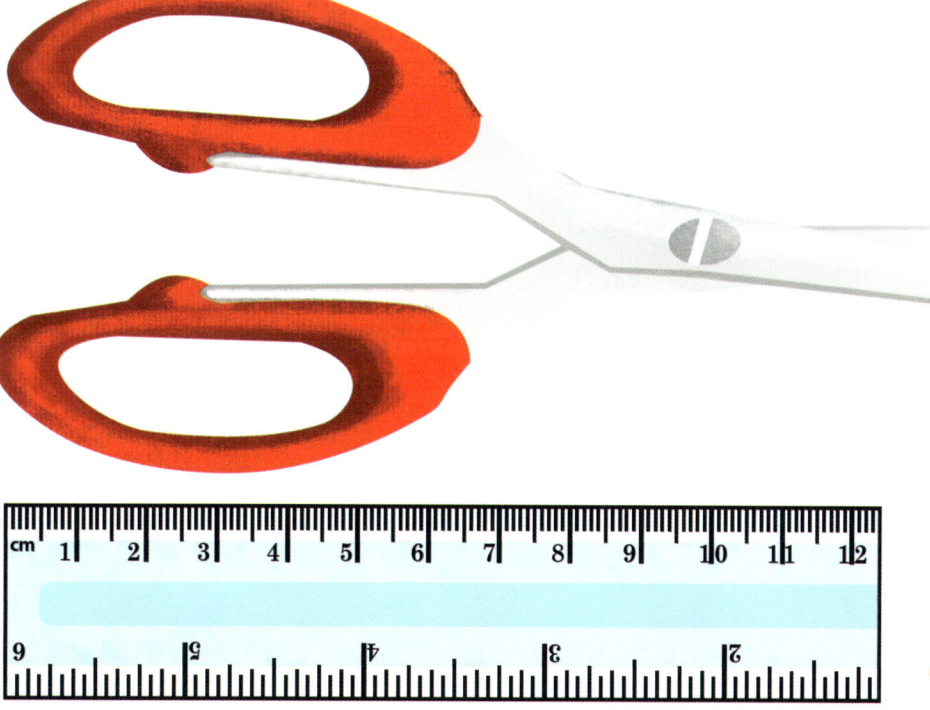

5 **Put stickers in your Picture dictionary: book, pencil, ruler, scissors.** On which page do the stickers belong? Find the correct page.

15

Starter unit

> 4 The alphabet

We are going to...
- **practise the letters of the alphabet.**

4 The alphabet

1 **The alphabet song**
Listen, point and sing along.

2 **An alphabet chant**
Listen, point and say.

1 Welcome to school

1.1 What do we do at school?

We are going to…
- say the name of things in our classroom.

Getting started

What do we do at school?

Look at the picture.
Point and say the words you know.

01 1 Making friends

Listen. How old are the children?

Practise the conversation with your partner.

2 Listen, point and say.

a table

a computer

a whiteboard

chairs

crayons

books

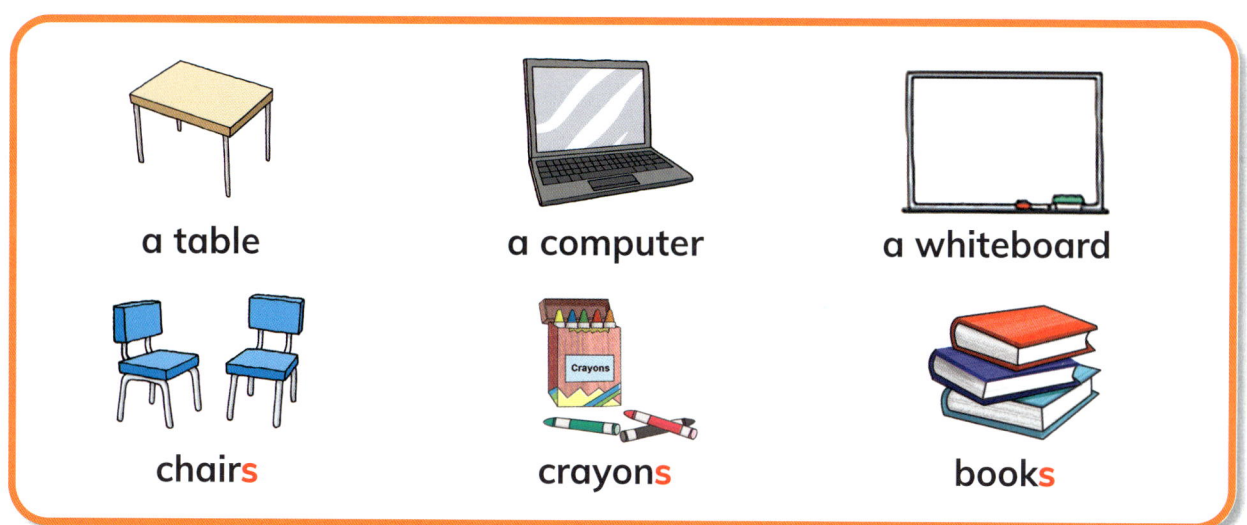

3 Look at the classroom.

Find:

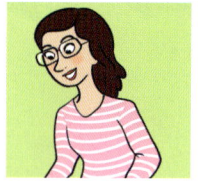

the teacher

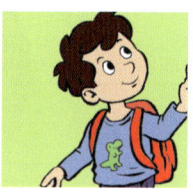

1 boy

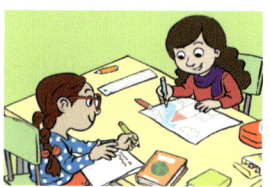

2 girls

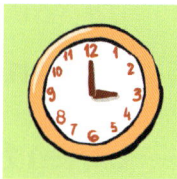

a clock

4 Read and listen.

Put the stickers on as you say the poem.

A [table] and [chairs],

A list of rules,

A [book] and [crayons],

Hello, school!

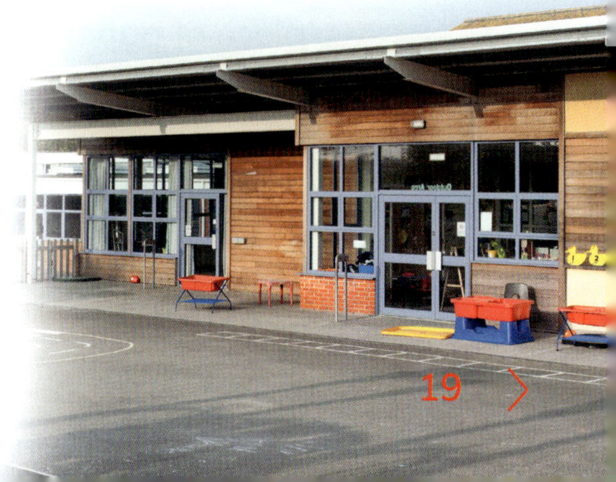

1 Welcome to school

> 1.2 In the classroom

We are going to…
- **name colours.**

a **red** ruler   a **blue** book

1   Read the colour words.

Name something in your classroom that is each colour.

red   orange
blue   black
green   purple
yellow   pink
brown   white

 2   Listen for information.

a   Fatima is talking with Ben. Listen. What questions does she ask?

b   Fatima talks with another friend. Listen. What is her name? What is her favourite colour?

Is it the **same** as Ben's favourite colour? Is it **different**?

3   Try this!

a   Draw your favourite colour on a piece of paper. 🔴

b   Ask a friend: **What's your favourite colour?** Draw the colour.

c   Look at the two colours. Are they the **same** or **different**?

Key words

same

different

20

1.2 Let's explore

4   Classroom treasure hunt

Matteo is doing a treasure hunt in his classroom.

Look and listen. Which thing is **not** in his classroom?

Now do a treasure hunt in your own classroom!

5   School poem

Read the poem in Lesson 1.

Write a new school poem with your class.

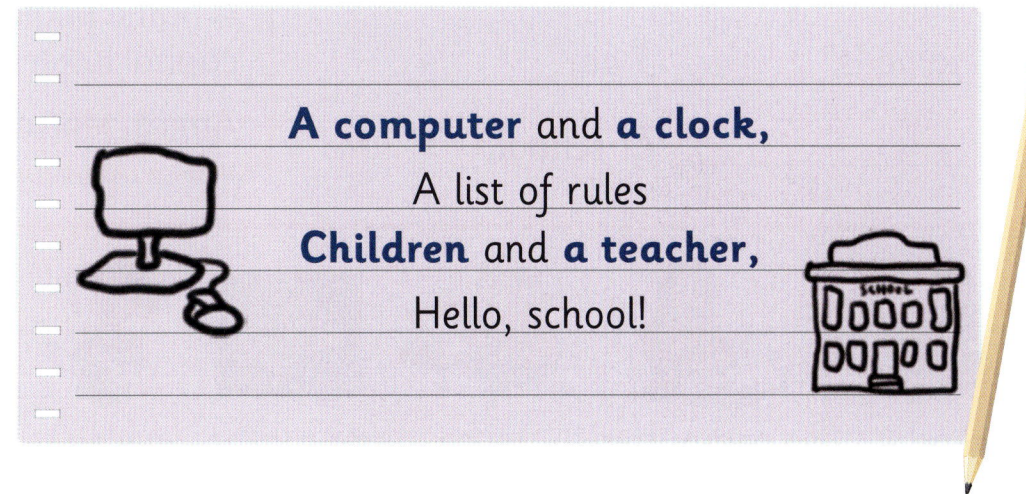

A computer and **a clock**,
A list of rules
Children and **a teacher**,
Hello, school!

1 Welcome to school

> 1.3 Children around the world

We are going to...
- talk and write about what we do in school.

 1 Before you read

Look at these photos.
What do the children do at school?
Listen and read.

My name is Marat. I am 7. I read at school.

Marat from Kazakhstan

My name is Amira. I am 6. I use computers at school.

Amira from Oman

My name is Zak. I am 6. I do maths at school.

Zak from New Zealand

2 What do you do at school?

Write about yourself. Draw a picture.

My name is _____. I am _____.

I _____ at school.

Writing tip

A name begins with a capital letter.

Amira, **M**arat, **Z**ak

Watch this!

 read    use computers    write    do maths    sing   draw

22

1.3 Global awareness

3   How do children go to school?

I go by bicycle.

We go by bus.

I go by car.

We go by boat.

We walk.

4   Put stickers in your Picture dictionary: bicycle, boat, bus, car.

On which page do the stickers belong? Find the correct page.

5   Make a class chart.

How do you go to school? Make a chart with your class.

How do you go to school?						
I go by bus.	Lara	Aron	Tanya	Ali	Paco	
I go by car.	Kuldip	Marta	Sara			
I go by bicycle.	Lucas					
I walk.	Pablo	Dina				

23

1 Welcome to school

> 1.4 This is my friend

We are going to...
- interview and introduce a friend.

1 Interview your partner.

Ask these questions. Write and draw the answers.

Can you spell your name, please?

How old are you?

What's your favourite colour?

2 Introduce your friend to the class.

This is my friend. **He** is a **boy**.
His name is _____.
He is _____.
His favourite colour is _____.

This is my friend. **She** is a **girl**.
Her name is _____.
She is _____.
Her favourite colour is _____.

Key word

interview:

Language detective

When do we say **he** and **his**? When do we say **she** and **her**?

1.4 Use of English

3 **Sing, move and point.**

The more we sing together

The more we sing together, together, together

The more we sing together, the happier we'll be.

First **he**  sings and **she**  sings.

Then **I**  sing; **we**  all sing!

The more we sing together, the happier we'll be.

4 **Choose a name card.**

Tell your partner about the child.
Can your partner guess who it is?

> This is a girl.
> Her name begins with R.
> Her favourite colour is red.

Name: Anna
Age: 6
Favourite colour: yellow

Name: Rosa
Age: 7
Favourite colour: red

Name: Tomas
Age: 7
Favourite colour: green

Name: Lan
Age: 8
Favourite colour: orange

5 **Make a name card. Play a game.**

Draw your face. Write your name, age and favourite colour.
Play a game with some of the name cards.
Choose a card.
Tell the class about the child. Can the class guess who it is?

1 Welcome to school

> 1.5 The alphabet

We are going to...
- read and write letters of the alphabet.

 1 Alphabet poem

Listen and point to the letters.

A B C D E F G
We're in school, you and me.

H I J K L M N
I have a pencil. You have a pen.

O P Q R S T
Look around. What do you see?

U V W X Y Z
Put your hands on your head!

2 Make a word wall.

What's the first letter of your name? Put your name under that letter.

1.5 Letters and sounds

3 **Sing a spelling song.**

Make 5 letter cards.

Point to the letters as you sing.

> **Bingo**
>
> There was a farmer had a dog
> And Bingo was its name-o.
> B-I-N-G-O!   B-I-N-G-O!   B-I-N-G-O!
> And Bingo was its name-o!

4 **Make a new song.**

Sing some new verses! Make letter cards. Point to the letters as you sing.

R E A D

S I N G

> Every day we read at school,   Every day we sing at school,
> We read with our teacher.   We sing with our teacher.
> R-E-A-D. R-E-A-D. R-E-A-D.   S-I-N-G. S-I-N-G. S-I-N-G.
> We read with our teacher.   We sing with our teacher.

1 Welcome to school

1.6 What do you see?

We are going to...
- read and talk about a poem.

 1 Listen and read.

What do you see?

Look left. Look right.

Look up and down.

What do you see when you look around?

On the way to school,
A surprise for you.
Tiny flowers, white and blue.

Reading tip

Look at the pictures.
What does the girl see on her way to school?

Birds in the sky.
Birds on the tree.
Birds we can hear, but cannot see.

Green, green grass.
Green, green leaves.
Look for some leaves that are NOT green.

1 Welcome to school

Up on the wall.
Do you see what I see?
A little lizard looking back at me!

1.6 Read and respond

2 **Act it out!**

Do the actions as you say this poem.

Look left. Look right.
Look up and down.

3 **Values:** It's a wonderful world.

How do you think the girl feels when she sees:

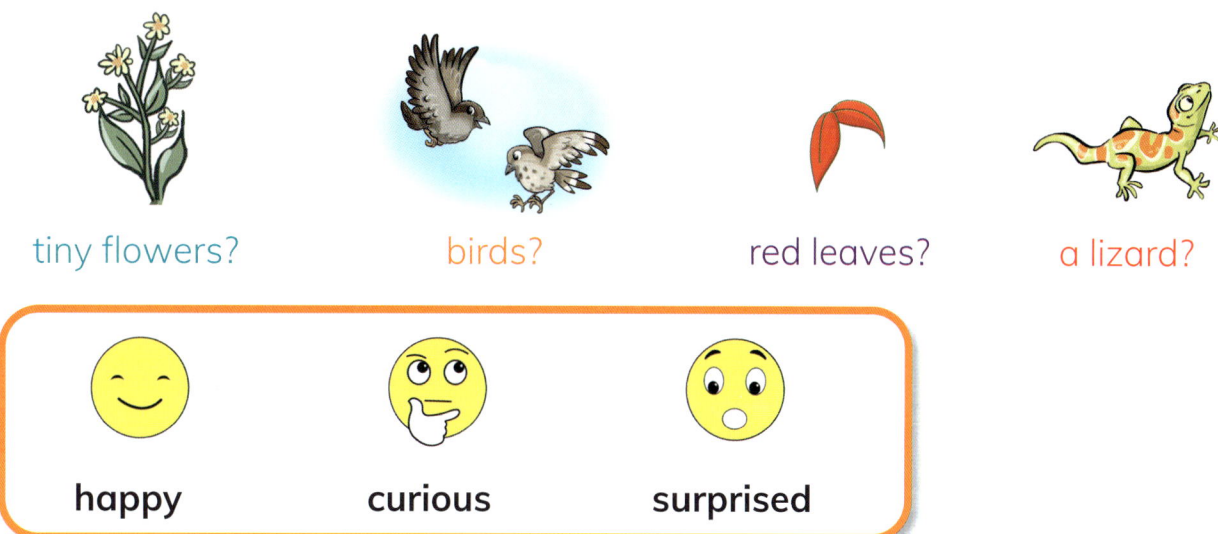

tiny flowers?   birds?   red leaves?   a lizard?

happy   curious   surprised

4 **What do you see on your way to school?**

Write about what you see and draw a picture.

On the way to school,

I see **flowers** and **a bee**.

I feel **curious**.

31

1 Welcome to school

> 1.7 Project challenge

Work with a partner or in a group. Work together to make the project. Then share the project with your class.

Project A: Make word cards

Write a word. Then draw a picture. What letter does the word begin with?

Add the word cards to the word wall. Teach your new words to the class.

car

table

Project B: Write a poem and draw a picture

What do you do at school?

Write a new poem with your friends.

Practise saying your poem. Then share it with your class.

School

We **read** at school

We **write** at school

We **draw** at school

School is cool!

1.7 Project challenge

Project C: Make a colour book or slideshow

Choose a colour – for example, red.

Draw pictures or take photos of things that are red.

Write words under each picture.

Share your project with the class.

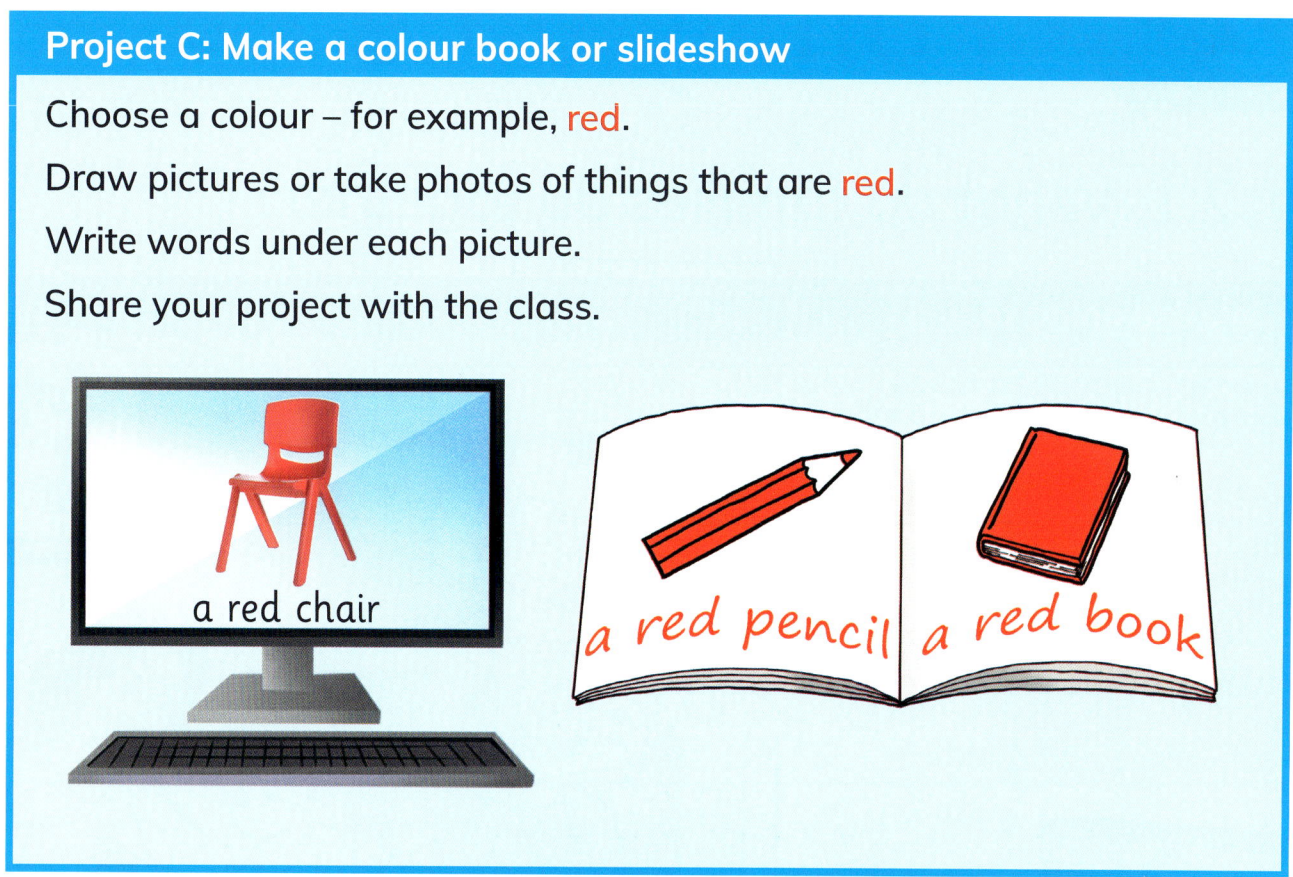

What is something new that you learned from this project?

Look what I can do!

I can say the name of things in our classroom.

I can name colours.

I can talk and write about what we do in school.

I can interview and introduce a friend.

I can read and write the letters of the alphabet.

I can read and talk about a poem.

2 Family time

> 2.1 What do families do together?

We are going to...
- talk about families.

Getting started

What do families do together?

Talk about what you know.
Look at the picture for some ideas.

1 Sam and his family

Sam is talking about his family.

What is everyone doing?

Watch this!

2.1 Think about it

 2 Listen, point and say.

3 The sound of th

Say the words mo**th**er, fa**th**er and bro**th**er.

What sound do you hear in the middle? What letters make the /th/ sound?

 4 Read and listen.

Put the stickers on as you say the poem.

What words in the poem rhyme with **mother**?

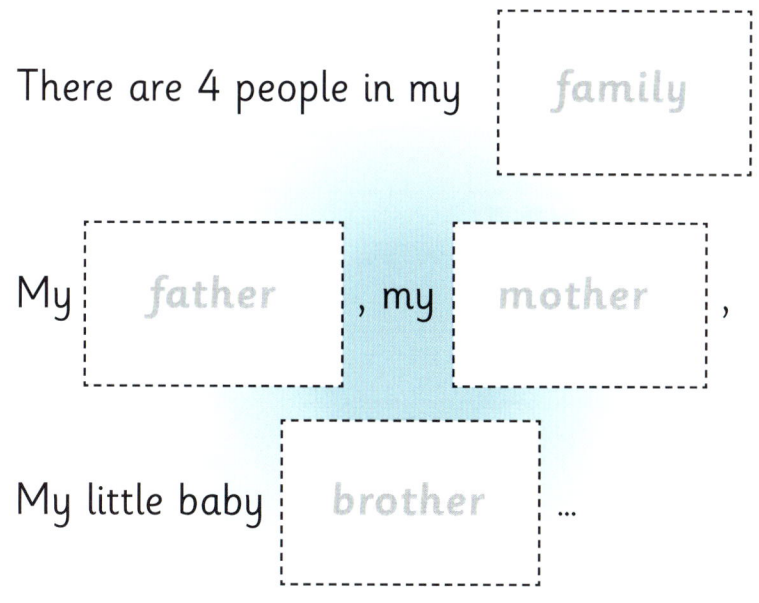

There are 4 people in my *family*.

My *father*, my *mother*,

My little baby *brother* …

Wait, there's one other… Oh, yes. It's me!

2 Family time

> 2.2 At home

We are going to...
- **talk about families.**

1 At home or at school?

Where do you do it? At home or at school?

a I talk with my teacher.

c I do maths with my class.

b I use a computer with my grandma.

d I sleep in my bed.

 2 Look at the pictures.

Listen, point and say.

eat dinner   dance   read books   play games   watch TV

2.2 Let's explore

3   Ask and answer questions.

What do you do with your family?
Talk with your partner.

Do you **read books** with your family?

Yes, I do.

No, I don't.

4   Read and match.

Who are the gifts for?

a   For Grandma

b   For my baby brother

c   For my big sister

I Love you GRANDMA

Sister

5   Make a card for your friend.

Draw a picture on the front.
Write a message inside.

Dear Ben,
Thank you for being my friend!

From,
Tom

This is for you.

For me? Thank you!

You're welcome.

37

2 Family time

> 2.3 Let's count!

We are going to...
- count and write numbers 0 to 10.

1 Put **stickers** in your Picture dictionary: **house**, door, **window**, bed.

On which page do the stickers belong? Find the correct page.

2 How many?

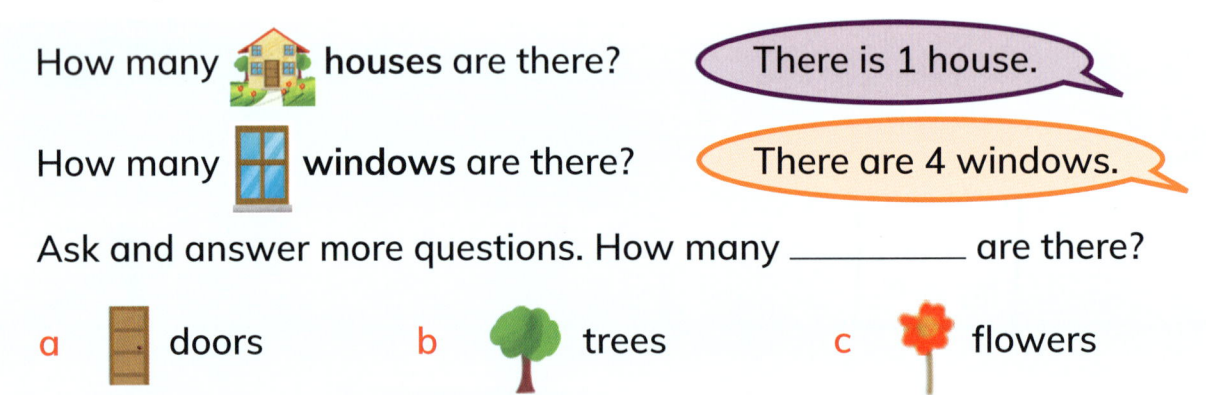

How many houses are there? — There is 1 house.

How many windows are there? — There are 4 windows.

Ask and answer more questions. How many _____ are there?

a doors   b trees   c flowers

3 Play a counting game.

Use a pencil and paper clip. Spin the paper clip.

Working in pairs, ask and answer questions. Take turns.

How many beds are there?

There are 2 beds

2.3 Maths

4 **Sing a counting song.**

Count and point from 0 to 10.

Then count **backwards**.

Listen to the song. Point to the number cards as you sing.

| 0 | 1 | 2 | 3 | 4 | 5 | 0 | 7 | 8 | 9 | 10 |
| zero | one | two | three | four | five | six | seven | eight | nine | ten |

Ten in the bed

There are **10** in the bed
And the little one says,
'Roll over. Roll over.'
So they all roll over and one falls out.

There are **9** in the bed
And the little one says,
'Roll over. Roll over.'
So they all roll over and one falls out.

. . .

There's **1** in the bed
And the little one says, 'Good night!'

5 **Sing the song in a new way.**

This time, sing: 'So they all roll over and **2** fall out.'

The last line of the song will be:

'There are zero in the bed and everyone says, Good night!'

Key word

zero = 0

0 birds = no birds

2 Family time

> 2.4 What do you eat for breakfast?

We are going to...
- **ask and answer questions about food.**

🎧 18   **1   Read, listen and say.**

> I eat noodles for breakfast.
> My brother eats eggs.

🎧 19   **2   Listen, point and say.**

What do you eat for breakfast?

Ask your partner.

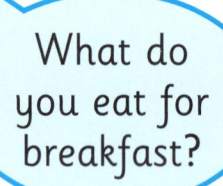

> What do you eat for breakfast?

rice    beans    eggs   bread

> I eat **bread**.

fruit    soup    noodles    yogurt

Language detective

I **eat** bread. Sami **eats** fruit.

Look at the two words in **red**. How are they different?

3   Write the answers.

What do you eat for breakfast? What does your partner eat?

I eat _____.   _____ eat**s** _____.

40

2.4 Use of English

4 **Listen and say the names of the fruit.**

Working in pairs, ask and answer questions.

apples   bananas   grapes   mangos   strawberries   pears

Do you like apples?

Yes, I do.

No, I don't

Tell the class what your partner likes and doesn't like.

Sara likes apples and grapes.
She doesn't like pears.

5 **Listen, sing and move.**

Sing new verses about the foods you like!

Bananas and mangos in my breakfast bowl
Keeps me happy all day.
Bananas and mangos in my breakfast bowl
Keeps the hungries away.
I open my mouth and down it goes.
Now I feel good from my head to my toes.
Bananas and mangos in my breakfast bowl
Keeps me happy all day.

6 **Do you like eggs?**

Look at the chart. How many children like eggs? _____
How many children don't like eggs? _____

Make your own class chart.

Do you like eggs?							
Yes, I do.	●	●	●	●	●	●	●
No, I don't.	●	●	●				

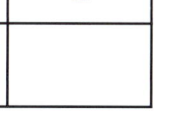

2 Family time

> 2.5 Short a

We are going to...
- read and write words with short a.

1 Listen, look and say.

Listen to the short a sound. Say the words.

apple   cat

2 Grandma's glasses

Listen to the rhyme. Say it.

Here are Grandma's glasses.

Here is Grandma's hat.

This is how she folds her hands

And puts them on her lap.

3 Say the rhyming words.

a   How are they the same? How are they different?

map    lap    nap

b   Here are two other words that rhyme with map. Spell and say these words.

c  _ _   c l _ _

42

2.5 Letters and sounds

4 **Read and listen.**

Act out what the cat does.

The cat

1

The cat has a hat.

2

The cat has a map.

3

The cat claps.

4

The cat is back.

5

The cat has a nap in Dad's lap.

Listen again. **Clap** when you hear a word with the short **a** sound.

2 Family time

2.6 Three families

We are going to...
- read and write about what families do.

Reading tip

Point to the picture of the shopping list.

Who is holding the shopping list in the big picture?

1 Listen and read.

Three families

All over the world, families work and have fun together.

Ayesha and her brother go shopping with Grandma.

Ayesha reads the shopping list.

What is in the shopping cart? What's next on the list?

- rice
- chicken
- carrots
- oranges
- milk

44

2.6 Read and respond

Kadar looks at his family's calendar.

Today is Saturday. Dad and Amira play with their boat.

Mum and Asha play music together.

Kadar goes out to meet his friends.

What do Kadar and his friends do?

Monday	Tuesday	Wednesday	Thursday	Friday	Saturday	Sunday
	Amira	Asha		Kadar	Amira Asha Kadar	

2 Family time

The Martinez family plans a party. Everyone helps.
Dad helps Paco make a birthday poster.
What does Mum do? What does Ana do?
Here's Grandpa! Everybody sings 'Happy birthday'.

- ☐ Make a cake
- ☐ Make birthday hats
- ☐ Make a birthday poster

HAPPY BIRTHDAY, GRANDPA!

2.6 Read and respond

2 Shopping lists

In the story, Ayesha's family uses a shopping list.

In pairs, write a shopping list of food you would like to buy.

rice
chicken
carrots
oranges
milk

3 Days of the week

Kadar's family uses a calendar.

What is your favourite day of the week? Why?

Sing a song about the days of the week!

4 Values: We love our families

Family time is fun! What do you and your family like to do together?

Talk about these ideas with your class. Think of some more ideas!

- We like to play games.
- We like to read.
- We like to watch TV.
- We like to go to the park.
- We like to run.
- We like to eat.
- We like to sing.
- We like to laugh.

5 Write and draw.

Draw something you and your family like to do together.

Write a sentence to go with the picture.

We like to eat ice cream.

Writing tip

A sentence begins with a capital letter.

Most sentences end with a full stop.

We like to sing.

2 Family time

> 2.7 Project challenge

Work with a partner or in a group to make the project.
Then share the project with your class.

Project A: Make a chart

Think of 3 questions: *Do you like…?*
Choose your favourite question.
Ask 10 people. Mark the answers on a chart.

Do you like bananas?
Yes, I do.

Do you like…?										
Yes, I do.										
No, I don't.										

Project B: Make a counting book

Take photos, draw, or use pictures from a computer.
Write words under each picture.

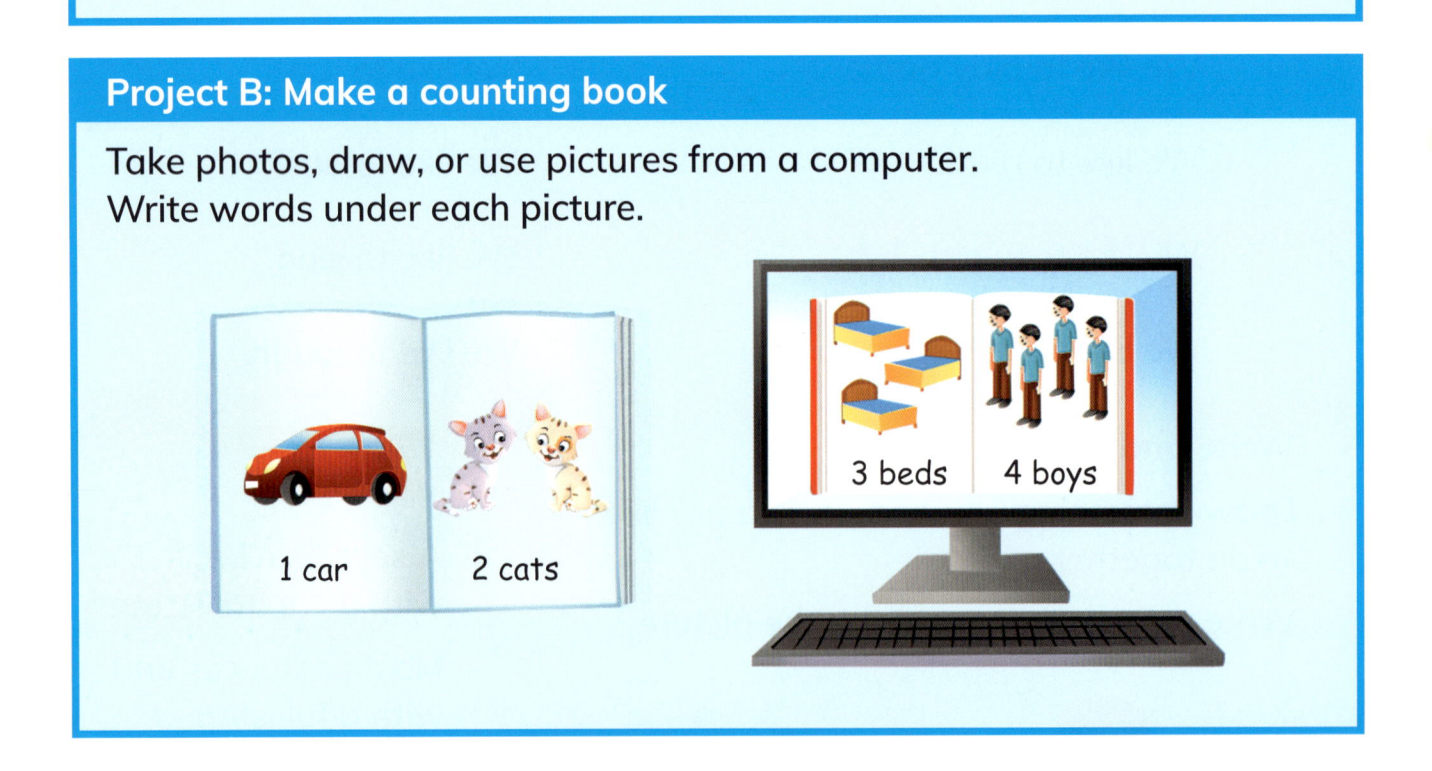

1 car   2 cats   3 beds   4 boys

2.7 Project challenge

Project C: Learn a poem

Read and learn this poem. Say and act out the words.
Make little chick stick puppets to act out the poem.

Good morning, Mother Hen

Chook, chook, chook, chook, chook.
Good morning, Mother Hen.
How many chicks have you got?
Oh my, I have 10.
4 of them are yellow.
4 of them are brown.
And 2 of them are speckled red,
The nicest in the town.

How did you help your group do the project?

Look what I can do!

I can talk about families.
I can count and write numbers from 0 to 10.
I can ask and answer questions about food.
I can read and write words with a short a.
I can read and write about what families do.

3 Fun and games

3.1 Let's have fun!

We are going to...
- **talk about things we can do.**

Getting started

What can we do for fun?

Talk about what you know.
Look at the picture for some ideas.

1 Listen and point.

Look at the children. Listen and point.

How many times can the girl bounce the ball?

Watch this!

50

3.1 Think about it

2 Listen, point and say.

Act it out!

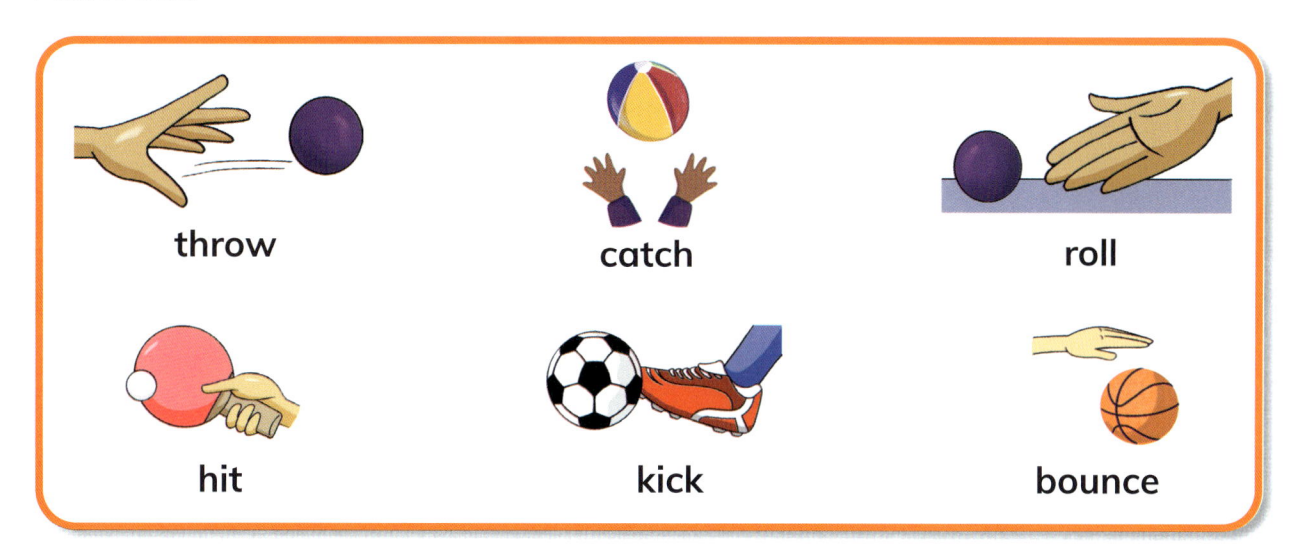

throw   catch   roll

hit   kick   bounce

3 Spelling

Listen and write the letters. What word do they spell?

4 Read and listen.

Put the stickers on as you say the poem. Act it out!

Ball, ball,

Bounce the ball!

Roll it, throw it,

Catch the ball!

51

3 Fun and games

3.2 Can you do it?

We are going to…
- **talk about things we can do.**

1 What can you do?

Work with a partner. Try these things.

Bounce a ball 4 times.

Throw a ball into a box.

Catch a ball with a box.

Roll a ball and hit a box.

Can you bounce a ball 4 times?

No, I can't.

Yes, I can.

Tell the class one thing **your partner** can do.

2 Draw and write.

Work with a partner.
What can you do with a ball and a box?

I can kick a ball.
I can hit a box.
I can _____.

3.2 Let's explore

3   Share the biscuits!

Cut out 12 pieces of paper.
Work in pairs.
Use these pieces to solve the problems!

| 1 | 2 | 3 | 4 | 5 | 6 |
| 7 | 8 | 9 | 10 | 11 | 12 |

a   There are 12 biscuits and 2 children.
How many biscuits can each child have?

b   There are 12 strawberries and 3 children.
How many strawberries can each child have?

c   There are 12 grapes and 4 children.
How many grapes can each child have?

4   Play a game.

You need a paper clip, pencil and your biscuits from Activity 3.

- Spin the paper clip.
- Take that number of biscuits.
- To win, you need 12 biscuits.

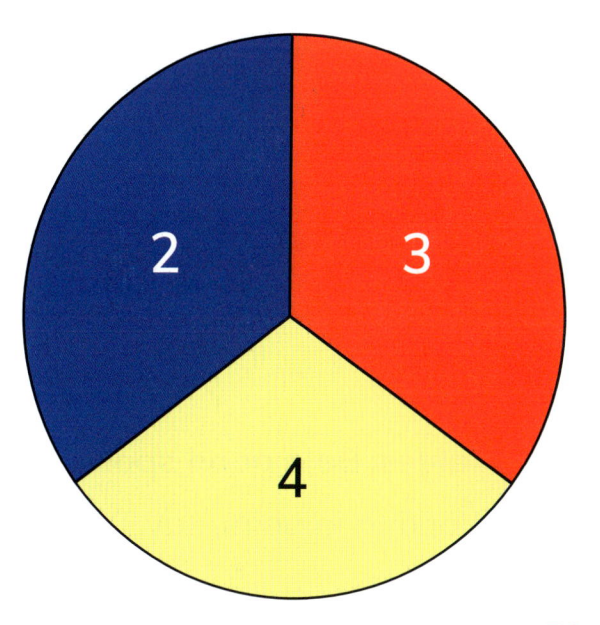

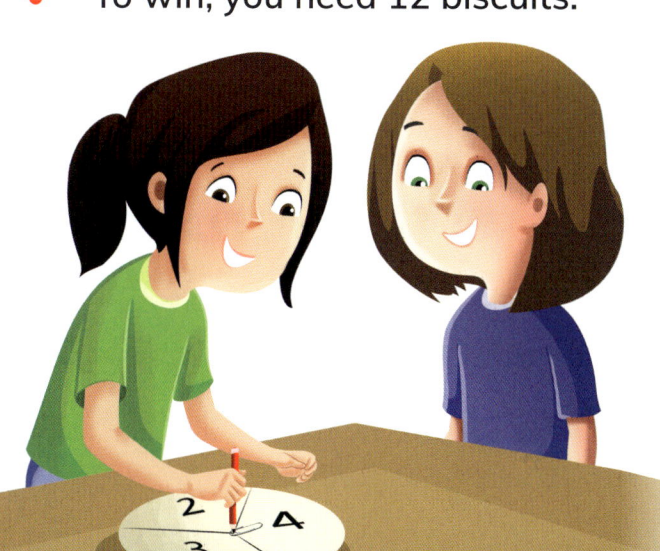

53

3 Fun and games

> 3.3 Games from around the world

We are going to...
- follow instructions and play games.

1 Listen and read.

Play 'Rock, paper, scissors'.

rock   paper   scissors

a   Face your partner. Say: '1, 2, 3, go!'
b   Make one of these signs with your hand: rock, paper, scissors.
c   Look at your partner's hand and your hand. Who wins the game?

paper   rock   Paper can cover a rock, so **paper** wins.

rock   scissors   A rock can break scissors, so **rock** wins.

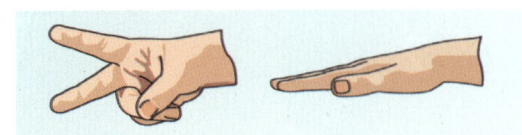

scissors   paper   Scissors can cut paper, so **scissors** win.

2 Values: Be a good sport!

Working in pairs, say, 'You win.' 'Well played!' and 'Let's play again.'

3.3 Global awareness

3 **Read and play.**

This game is called 'Bird, water, rock', and is from Malaysia.

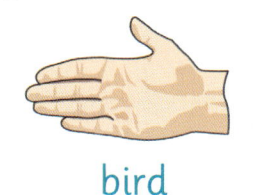

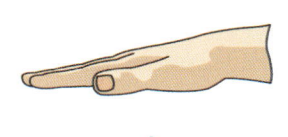

bird   water   rock

a   Face your partner. Say: '1, 2, 3, go!'
b   Make one of these signs with your hand: bird, water, rock.
c   Look at your partner's hand and your hand. Who wins the game?

bird   water   A bird can drink water, so **bird** wins.

water   rock   Water can cover a rock, so _____.

rock   bird   A rock can hit a bird, so _____.

4 **Compare the games.**

How are these two games the same?
How are they different?

Key word

compare

3 Fun and games

> 3.4 Where is the duck?

We are going to...
- say where things are

1 Ask and answer questions.

Point to a picture.
Ask your partner a question.

Where is the duck?

The duck is **on** the table.

a  on

b under

c next to

Language detective

Where is her pencil?
Her pencil is _____ her nose.

Where is his pencil?
His pencil is _____ his shoulder.

3.4 Use of English

2 **Play an instructions game.**

Play this game with your class. Take turns giving instructions.

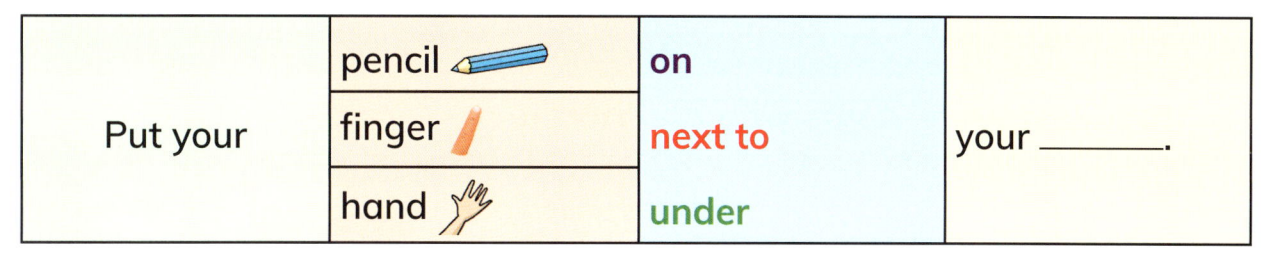

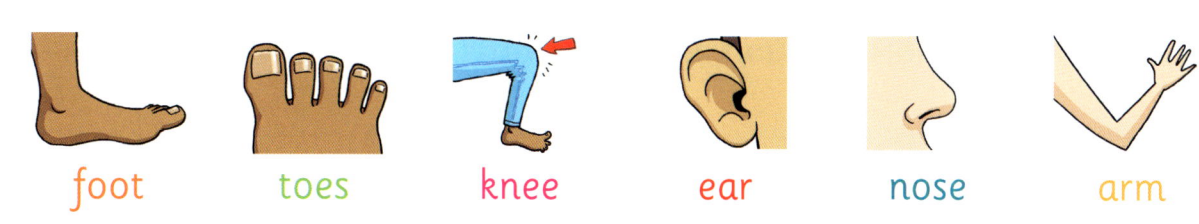

Put your	pencil	on	your _____ .
	finger	next to	
	hand	under	

foot   toes   knee   ear   nose   arm

3 **Wind the bobbin up.**

Follow the instructions. Sing and dance!

Chorus:
Wind the bobbin up.
Wind the bobbin up.
Pull, pull. Clap, clap, clap.

Point to **your shoulders**.
Point to **your nose**.
Point to **your ears** and
Point to **your toes**.
Clap your hands together, 1, 2, 3.
Put your hands upon your knees.

Repeat chorus.
Point to **the ceiling**.
Point to **the floor**.
Point to **the window** and
Point to **the door**.
Clap your hands together, 1, 2, 3.
Put your hands upon your knees.

ceiling

floor

4 **Write a new verse of the song.**

Teach your new verse to a partner or your class.

3 Fun and games

> 3.5 Short u

We are going to...
- read and write words with the short u.

🎧 35 **1 Listen, look and say.**

Listen to the short u sound. Say the words.

cup   bug

🎧 36 **2 Listen to the poem. Act it out!**

I can run like a puppy!
I can jump like a bug!
I can buzz like a bee!
I can sit on the rug.

3 Tic-tac-toe: a or u?

Player 1: Write a on 5 letter cards. Find a gameboard space that has a word with the short a sound. Read the word and put a letter card on that space.

Player 2: Write u on 5 letter cards. Find a space that has a word with the short u sound. Read the word and put a letter card on that space.

Take turns with your partner. To win, put 3 cards in a row.

The cat can cut.	clap	A fan is fun!
run	a bug on a bag	nut
a cup and a cap	dad	Mud makes me mad!

a a a a a

u u u u u

58

3.5 Letters and sounds

4   Phonics story

Listen and read. Put your hand **up** when you hear a word with the short **u** sound. Then, act out the story!

Run, duck, run!

1

I run in the sun. It's lots of fun!

This duck runs.
Run, duck, run!

2

Help! I'm stuck in the mud!

I can help. I have a truck.

The duck is in the mud.
She's stuck!

3

Up, up, up!

Thank you very much!

The duck goes up.

4

Good luck!

Goodbye.

The muddy duck runs again.

**5   Put stickers in your Picture dictionary:
clap, cut, jump, run.**

On which page do the stickers belong?
Find the correct page.

59

3 Fun and games

> 3.6 The Ker-PLUNK

We are going to...
- read, talk about and act out a play.

Reading tip

In this play, the small pictures in boxes show who is talking.

Look at the pictures. Who are the characters in this play?

1 Listen and read.

The Ker-PLUNK

A story from China

A rabbit is having a nap next to a pond.
The rabbit hears a strange and scary sound. Ker-PLUNK!

Help! A scary Ker-PLUNK! Run, run, run!

What's wrong, Rabbit?

It's the scary Ker-PLUNK! Hurry!

Oh, no! A scary Ker-PLUNK! Flap, flap, flap!

Run, run, run!

Watch this!

3.6 Read and respond

What's wrong? What's wrong?

It's the scary Ker-PLUNK! Hurry!

Oh, no! A scary Ker-PLUNK! Jump, jump, jump!

Flap, flap, flap!

Run, run, run!

STOP! What's wrong?

It's the scary Ker-PLUNK!

It's very scary!

Very scary!

What's a Ker-PLUNK?

I don't know.

3 Fun and games

Just then, a big nut falls from a tree into the pond. Ker-PLUNK!

Help! A scary Ker-PLUNK! Run, run, run!

Silly rabbit! A big nut fell in the pond. It made the sound Ker-PLUNK.

What? Is the Ker-PLUNK a nut?

Yes.

That's not scary.

No.

Oh, well. Let's go home.

Goodbye, wise lion!

Goodbye, silly animals. Good luck!

3.6 Read and respond

2 **Explore the characters.**

a Why is Rabbit scared?

b What makes the sound, Ker-PLUNK?

c _____ and _____ and _____ are silly.

d _____ is wise.

3 **Act out the play!**

Which character will you be?

4 **Values: Feelings**

Oh, no! Rabbit is scared!

a How do you think Rabbit looks when he is scared? Act it out!

b What do the ducks and the frogs say to Rabbit?

c Rabbit thinks the Ker-PLUNK is very scary.
    Which of these things do **you** think are scary?

A storm   A train    A fire    A lion

5 **Write and draw.**

a Why is Rabbit scared?

b Write the word in the comic strip and draw a picture.

c What can you say to Rabbit so he feels better? Write sentences from the box or use your own ideas.

| Don't be scared, Rabbit. | I'm here with you. |
| A _____ is not scary. | Let's go look at it. |

63

3 Units 1–3: Review

> 3.7 Project challenge

Work with a partner or in a group.
Then share the project with your class.

Project A: Write clues for a treasure hunt

Find 3 places in your classroom to hide clues – **on**, **under** or **next to** things.

Write the 3 clues. Use words and pictures.

Make a 'You have found the treasure!' picture too.

Play treasure hunt with your class.

- Hide clues 2 and 3 and the 'You have found the treasure!' picture in the correct places.
- Then read the first clue to the class. Can they find the next clue?

1 Look on the

2 Look next to the

3 Look under a

Project B: Make a 'Parts of the body' poster

Draw hair, eyes, ears, nose and a mouth on a big body shape.

Write words for parts of the body.

Read the words to your class.

Then play 'Point to knee' with the paper body.

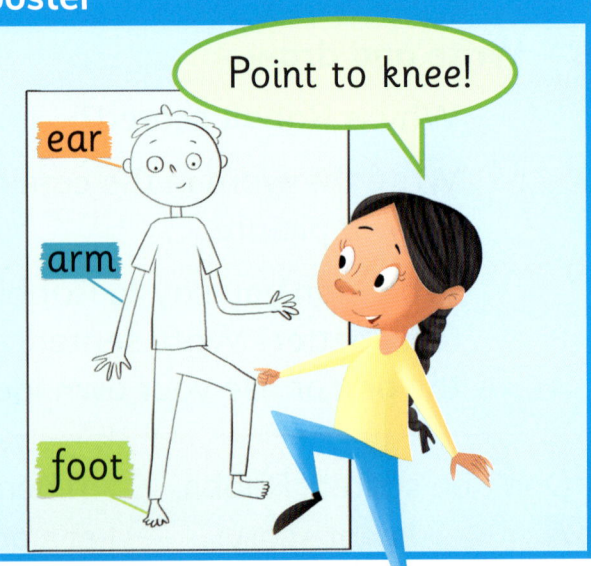

Point to knee!

ear
arm
foot

3.7 Project challenge

Project C: Make up a clapping game

Think up a clapping pattern. For example:

| clap | right hands | clap | left hands | clap | right hands |

Here are some other moves you can include:

| both hands | knees | shoulders | head |

Teach your hand-clapping game to the class.

What is something new that you learned from this project?

Look what I can do!

I can talk about things I can do.

I can follow instructions and play games.

I can read and write words with the short **u**.

I can say where things are (**on**, **next to**, **under**).

I can read, talk about and act out a play.

65

3 Units 1–3: Review

› Check your progress

Let's go to the park!

We can go to the park by bicycle, by bus, or by car!

You need:
- 2 to 3 players
- a different game marker for each player
- number cards.

1	1	1	1
2	2	2	2
3	3	3	3

Directions

Step 1. Take a number card.

Step 2. Count and move your game marker on the game track. Then do one of these things:
- Read the **word** or the **clue**. Go to the matching picture.
- Look at the picture. Say the word.
- Read and follow the **directions**.

Step 3. The first player to get to the park is the winner!

START

1 — cat

2 — Say 'hello' to your friends.

13 — Go up!

14 — cut

15

Check your progress: Let's go to the park!

20	(car)
19	bus
18	(bicycle)
17	(cutting)
16	Clap your hands.
12	It can jump.
11	Count to 12.
10	(goose)
9	This bird has 2 legs.
8	(boy running)
7	duck
6	Spell your name.
5	He can run.
4	(cat with hat)
	has a hat.

67

4 Making things

> 4.1 What are they wearing?

We are going to...
- talk about what people are wearing and making.

Getting started

Who is taking part in the fun day?

Look at the picture for some ideas.

🎧 39 1 We're going to a fun day!

Listen to Lucy. Her family is going to a fun day.

Point to Lucy. What is each person dressed in?

4.1 Think about it

2   Listen, point and say.

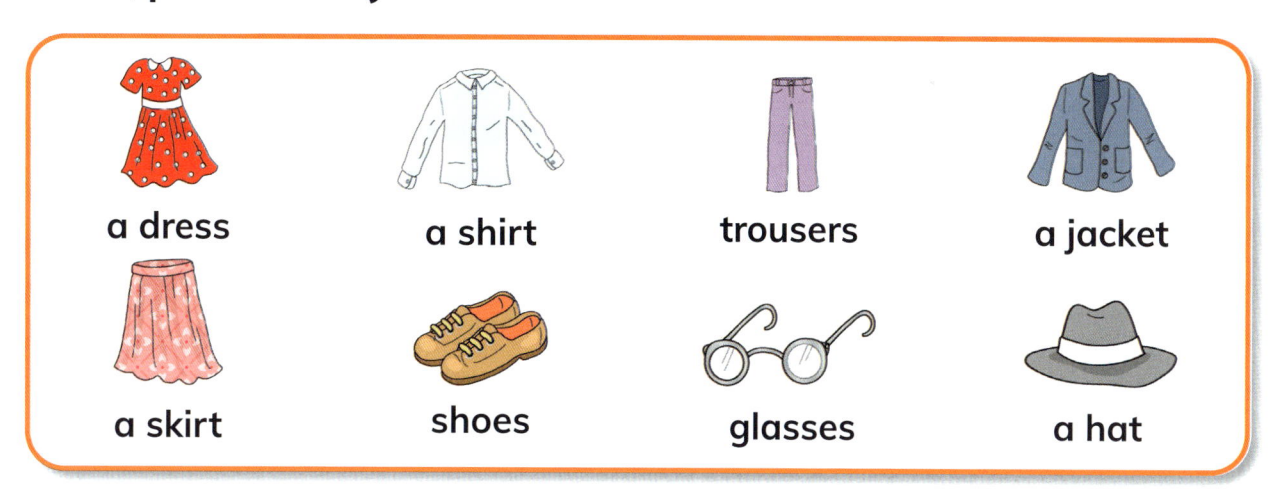

a dress   a shirt   trousers   a jacket

a skirt   shoes   glasses   a hat

3   Who are you?

Working in pairs, pretend you are going to the fun day.
Tell your partner what you are wearing. Ask 'Who am I?'
Can your partner guess who you are?

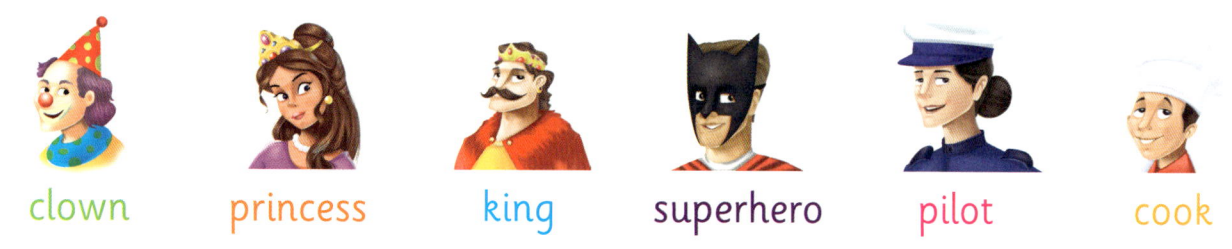

clown   princess   king   superhero   pilot   cook

4   Read and listen.

Put the stickers on as you say the poem.

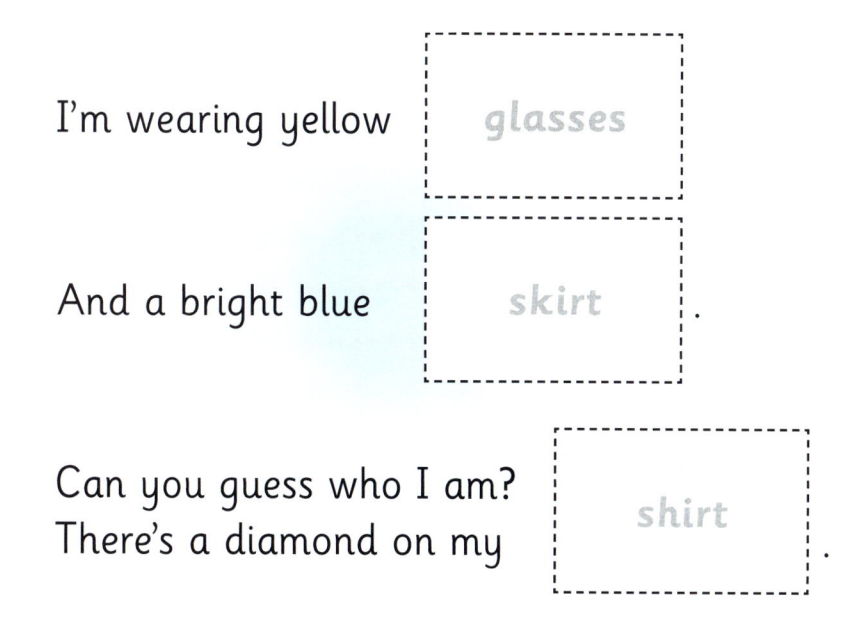

I'm wearing yellow   glasses

And a bright blue   skirt   .

Can you guess who I am?
There's a diamond on my   shirt   .

4 Making things

> 4.2 Making puppets

We are going to…
- talk about what people are wearing and making.

1 Family fun

The families are making puppets.

Some families are using socks and gloves.
Some families are using big spoons.

Listen, point and count.

0 1 2 3 4 5
6 7 8 9 10 11
12 13 14 15

How many spoons are there?

I am making a clown puppet.

What are you making?

Make a puppet from big spoon

Make a puppet from a glove

Make a puppet from a sock

How many socks?

How many gloves?

4.2 Let's explore

2   Look at the pictures.

Listen and say.

Find the 2 pictures that go with each sentence.

I'm making a crown for my puppet.

I'm making glasses for my puppet.

I'm making a skirt for my puppet.

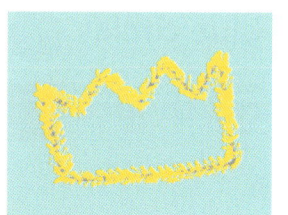

Writing tip

When we say 'I **am**', the words join together. We write it like this: **I'm**.

When we say 'He **is**', the words join together. We write it like this: **He's**.

3   Draw and write.

What clothes are you making for your puppet? Draw and write a sentence.

I'm making _____ for my puppet.

4 Making things

> 4.3 Colourful quilts with shapes

We are going to...
- talk about shapes
- count to 20.

circle
rectangle
square
triangle

1 Find and count the shapes.

This colourful blanket is called a quilt.

Work in pairs. Look for different shapes in the quilt.

a How many blue **rectangles** can you see? _____

b How many red **triangles** can you see? _____

c How many red **squares** can you see? _____

d How many blue **circles** can you see? _____

e How many red **shapes** can you see? _____

Language tip

We use **and** to link words and phrases:
blue and green.

2 Read and listen.

What are the missing words?

Mei Mei likes red, black _____ white.
She's cutting squares and _____.

Kevin likes orange, purple _____ green.
He's cutting triangles and _____.

72

4.3 Maths

3 Paper shapes

Look at the girls.
They are cutting green triangles.
What is the boy saying?

4 Making things with paper shapes

What are the children making?
Read and find out.

We're cutting green triangles.

The boy is making a paper quilt with rectangles.
How many rectangles is he using?

This girl is making a picture with her shapes.
How many triangles is she using?

5 It's your turn!

Cut some paper shapes and make a paper quilt or a picture.

Talk to your partner.
Ask and answer questions.

What are you doing?

I'm cutting blue squares.
I'm making a picture.

73

4 Making things

> 4.4 Painting a mural

We are going to...

- talk and write about what people are doing.

1 Look and listen.

Liz and her friends are making a mural. Listen and point to Liz.

Look at the sentences and say the missing words.

a   The children _____ painting a picture.

b   Liz _____ _____ a red jet.

c   Emily and Ava _____ _____ a gold bridge.

d   Tina _____ cutting silver stars.

e   The teacher is _____ painting.

f   Liz thinks the city is _____.

4.4 Use of English

2 What are they wearing?

Working in pairs, say what clothes the people are wearing in the picture.

Tina   Liz   Marcos and Rob

Emily and Ava   the teacher

Language detective

We use **is** to talk about one person. We use **are** to talk about more than one person.

Which sentence uses **is** and which uses **are**?

Marcos and Rob _____ wearing red.

Tina _____ wearing purple.

3 Listen to the song.

Sing it with your class and do the actions.

London Bridge is falling down,
Falling down, falling down.
London Bridge is falling down,
My fair lady.

Build it up with **silver** and **gold**,
Silver and **gold**, **silver** and **gold**.
Build it up with **silver** and **gold**,
My fair lady.

4 Make a new version.

Sing some new verses using the colours you like.

What building will you choose? Maybe your school!

We are painting the school house,
The school house, the school house.
We are painting the school house,
My fair lady.

We can paint it **red** and **gold**,
Red and **gold**, **red** and **gold**.
We can paint it **red** and **gold**,
My fair lady.

4 Making things

> 4.5 Short e

We are going to...
- read and write words with a short e.

1 Listen, look and say.

Listen to the short e sound.
Say the words.

egg    pen

2 Rhyming words

Can you find the rhyming words in picture a and picture b?

Make a rhyme for picture c.

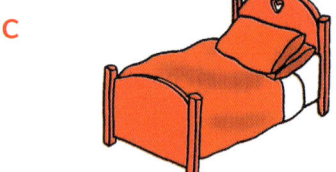

a   b   c

The hen has a pen.   Meg has an egg.   _____

3 Listen to the rhyme.

Say it and write the missing words.

Higgledy Piggledy
My black hen
She lays _____
For gentlemen.
Sometimes nine and sometimes _____.
Higgledy Piggledy
My black _____.

4.5 Letters and sounds

4 Read and listen.

How many words do you hear with the short **e** sound?

The tent

1 Let's make a tent.

2 Look! A red tent next to the bed.

3 Let's put the teddy in the tent.

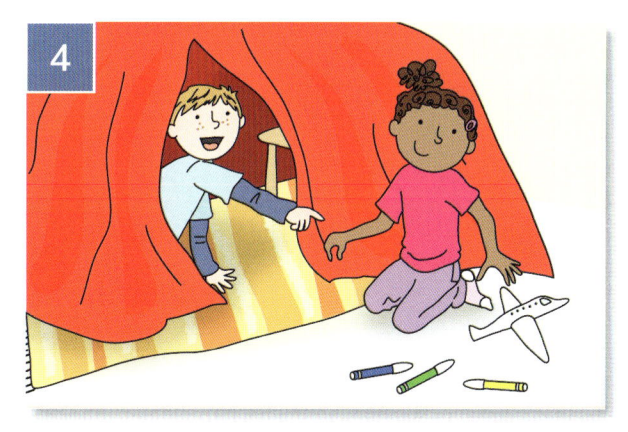

4 Let's put the jet in the tent.

5 Let's put the ten pens in the tent.

6 This tent is the best!

I like this tent!

4 Making things

4.6 The Elves and the Shoemaker

We are going to...
- **read, talk about and act out a story.**

Reading tip

As you read, think about these questions:
- How do the elves help the shoemaker?
- How does the shoemaker help the elves?

1 **Listen and read.**

Watch this!

The Elves and the Shoemaker

A story from Germany

1 I'm very tired.

The shoemaker is making shoes.

2 Let's help the shoemaker.

The shoemaker is sleeping.
The elves are making the shoes.

4.6 Read and respond

It's morning.
The shoemaker wakes up.

The shoemaker is selling the shoes.

The shoemaker is very tired.
The elves are working.
The shoemaker is not sleeping. He is watching.

4 Making things

6 "How can I thank the elves?"

"Look at these pretty shoes!"

The shoemaker is selling more shoes.
He wants to thank the elves.

7

The shoemaker is making a present for the elves.

8 "New boots! New jackets! New hats!"

"Look at our lovely clothes!"

The elves are happy.
The shoemaker is happy too.

4.6 Read and respond

2 **Think about the story.**

What is the title of the story?

Who are the characters in this story?

Look at the story pictures. How are the elves helping the shoemaker?

3 **Values:** **Saying thank you**

The shoemaker makes a 'thank you' present for the elves. What does he make?

What present would you choose for your teacher to say thank you?

4 **Write a thank you note.**

Imagine you are one of the elves.
Write a thank you letter to the shoemaker.

5 **Puppets**

Working in pairs, make some puppets.
Act out the story.

6 **Clothes in the pictures**

Find these clothes in the pictures.

| jacket | trousers | dress |
| shirt | hat | shoes |

Language detective

Look at page 80. Find 2 words that mean the same as **beautiful**.

7 **Put stickers in your Picture dictionary:**
shoes, boots, jacket, hat.

On which page do the stickers belong? Find the correct page.

4 Making things

> 4.7 Project challenge

Work with a partner or group to make the project.
Then share the project with your class.

Project A: Make a fashion model

Cut out and colour the clothes.

What is your model wearing?

- Draw or find pictures on the computer.
- Name your fashion model.
- Discuss your fashion model with a friend.

> My model is wearing black trousers and a blue jacket.

Project B: Make a shape animal

Use triangles, rectangles, squares, circles and diamonds.

Write about your shape animal.

Can your friends find the shapes?

One person can make the body and the other the head out of shapes.

Can you find these shapes?

- 2 yellow circles
- 1 brown diamond
- 2 orange triangles
- 2 blue circles

4.7 Project challenge

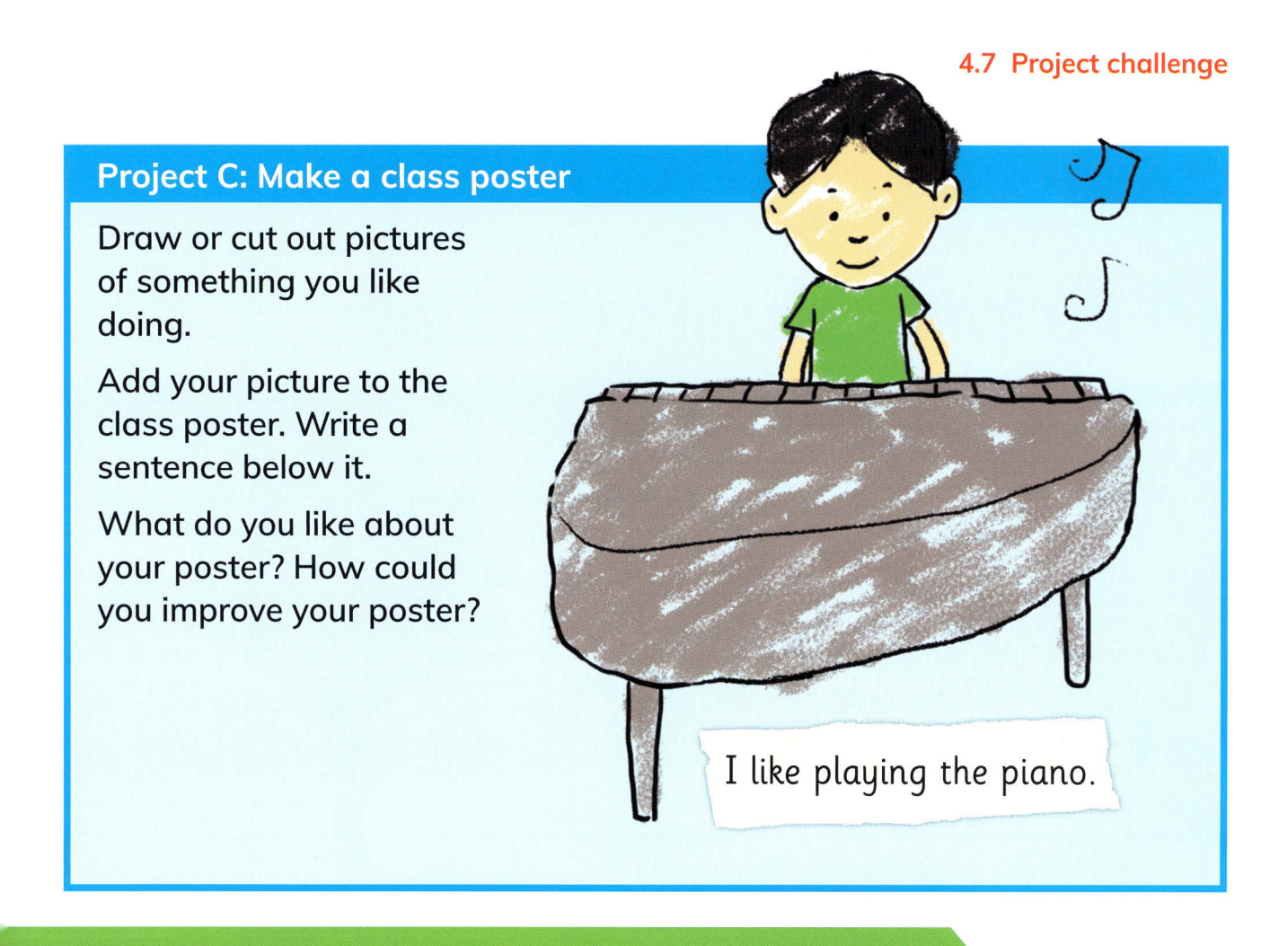

Project C: Make a class poster

Draw or cut out pictures of something you like doing.

Add your picture to the class poster. Write a sentence below it.

What do you like about your poster? How could you improve your poster?

I like playing the piano.

How did you help share your project with the class?

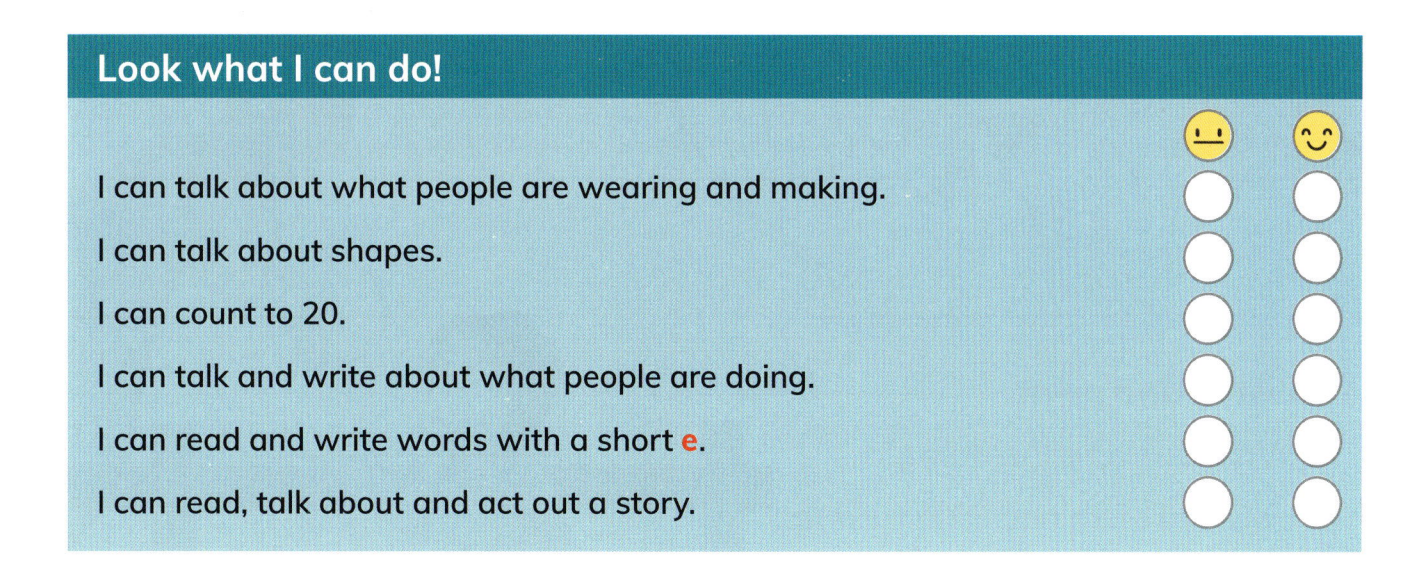

Look what I can do!

I can talk about what people are wearing and making.

I can talk about shapes.

I can count to 20.

I can talk and write about what people are doing.

I can read and write words with a short **e**.

I can read, talk about and act out a story.

5 > On the farm

> 5.1 What can you find on a farm?

We are going to...
- name things on a farm.

Getting started

What can you find on a farm?
Look at the picture for some ideas.

1 Listen and point.
What is everyone doing?
Listen to Mum and Dina talking.
Practise with your partner.

Watch this!

5.1 Think about it

2   Listen, point and say.

tractor   cow   sheep   hen   horse   goat

3   Listen and write the letters.

What word do they spell?

4   Here or there?

Listen and fill in the missing word in each sentence.

a   _____ is my horse. I'm feeding her an apple.

b   _____'s an apple for you too, goat!

c   Our lambs are over _____, under the tree.

5   Read and listen.

Put the stickers on as you say the poem.
Act it out!

Hello to the farmer on his   tractor .

Hello to the   cow   in her stall.

Hello to the   sheep , hello to the   hens .

Hello, hello to you all!

85

5 On the farm

> 5.2 Living on the farm

We are going to...
- talk about what people are doing.

1   Interviews with farm families

Listen and find the correct picture. Practise the conversations.

a    feeding   b    carrying   c    picking   d    driving   e    planting

2   What are they doing?

Look at the pictures. Say the sentences. Fill in the missing words.

a   They are _____ seeds.

b   She is _____ strawberries.

c   He ___ _____ a tractor.

d   They ___ _____ lambs.

86

5.2 Let's explore

3 Act it out.

Act out one of the sentences in activity 2.
Can your partner guess what you are doing?

Are you picking 🍓?

No, I'm not.

Are you planting 🫘?

Yes, I am!

4 Read and listen.

Living things

On a farm, there are animals and plants.
Animals are living things. Plants are living things too.
Living things need food and water to grow.
Little animals grow. They become big animals.
Little plants grow. They become big plants.

5 Living or non-living?

Which **three** are living things?

a   b   c   d   e   f

5 On the farm

> 5.3 Life cycles

We are going to...
- learn about how plants and animals grow and change.

Reading tip

Diagrams help to show information clearly.

Look at the diagram of the life cycle of a bean. Follow the arrows.

Can you explain what happens?

Key word

diagram

1 Listen and read.

The life cycle of a bean

- A seed is planted in the ground.
- The seed starts to grow.
- The seed grows into a plant.
- A bean grows on the plant.
- The bean has seeds.

88

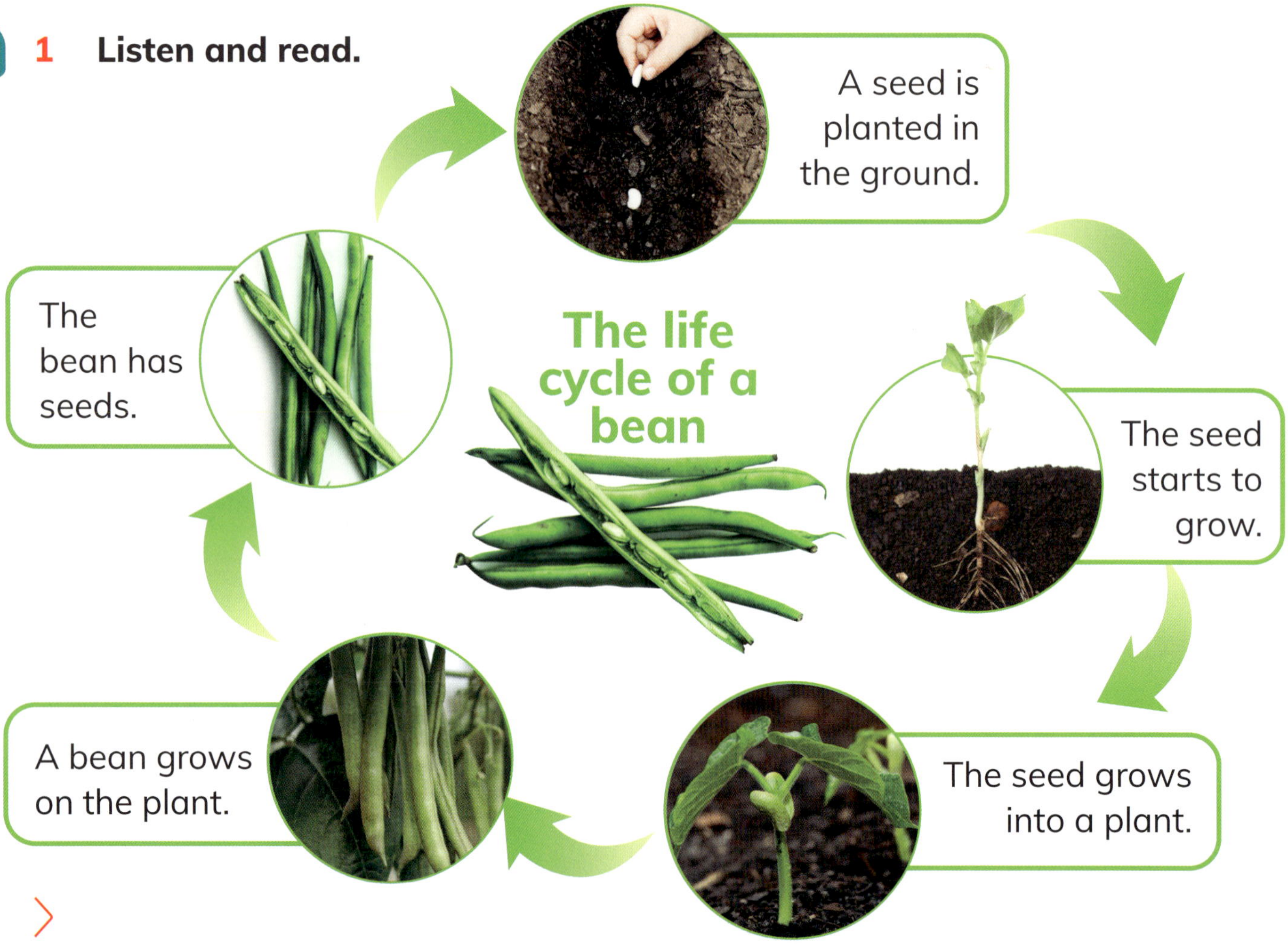

5.3 Science

2 Which three things grow from seeds?

Talk with a partner.

a   b   c   d   e

3 Listen and read.

The life cycle of a hen

A tiny chick grows inside an egg.

The chick comes out of the egg.

The yellow chick eats and grows.

The chick becomes a hen. The hen lays an egg.

4 Draw and write.

A baby duckling grows into a duck.
Make a diagram: 'The life cycle of a duck'.
Use 'The life cycle of a hen' as a model.

egg   duckling   duck

5 On the farm

5.4 What is happening on the farm?

tomatoes   peppers   beans

We are going to...
- ask and answer questions.

carrots onions potatoes

1 **Where are the vegetables growing?**

Are they **above** the ground or **in** the ground?

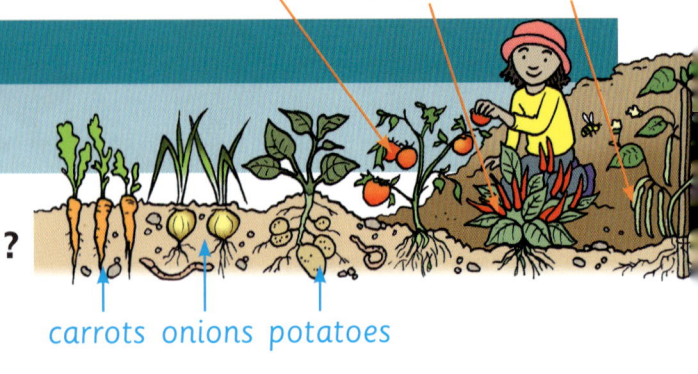

2 **Put your stickers in your Picture dictionary:**
carrot, pepper, onion, potato.

On which page do the stickers belong? Find the correct page.

Language detective

Fill in the missing words.

they + ____ = **they're**

she + ____ = **she's**

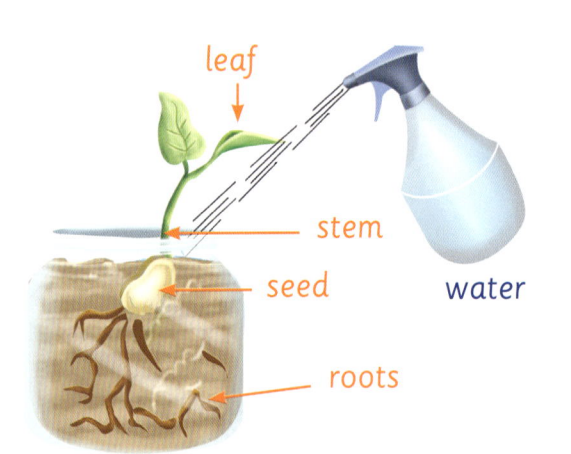

3 **Ask and answer questions.**

a   Are the carrots growing above the ground?
Yes, they are.   **No, they're not.**

b   Is the girl picking peppers?
Yes, she is.   **No, she's not.**

leaf
stem
seed
roots
water

4 **Grow a bean plant.**

Put a bean seed in a jar or plastic bag. Draw and write about your growing plant.

5 **Ask and answer questions.**

In pairs, look at the diagram.

a	Is the seed dry?	**Yes, it is.**	**No, it's not.**
b	Are the roots green?	**Yes, they are.**	**No, they're not.**
c	Is the stem straight?	**Yes, it is.**	**No, it's not.**

5.4 Use of English

6   Listen to the animals.

Point to each animal as you hear it.

Ask and answer questions.

What is the sheep saying?

moo, cluck, quack, neigh, meow, baa, woof

7   Sing the song!

Old MacDonald had a farm
Old MacDonald had a farm, E-I-E-I-O.
And on that farm he had a cow, E-I-E-I-O.
With a moo moo here and a moo moo there,
Here a moo, there a moo, everywhere a moo moo!
Old MacDonald had a farm, E-I-E-I-O.

verse 1

verse 2

8   Sing some new verses.

Draw and write the name of a farm animal on a card.

Put the cards together.

Pick a card and sing a verse about that animal.

verse 3

5 On the farm

> 5.5 Short i

We are going to...

- read and write words with the short **i**.

1 Listen, look and say.

Listen to the short **i** sound. Say the words.

big   pick

Add the short **i** sound to make the name of this animal.

Listen to the sound of **ch** in chick.   ch_ck

Can you think of two more words beginning with **ch**? The picture will help you.

2 Tongue twisters

A tongue twister is very difficult to say. It twists your tongue! Say each tongue twister three times. Have fun!

Six sisters sing to six sick sheep.

How many sticks can a big chick kick?

Little lambs like leaping over logs.

5.5 Letters and sounds

3 Read and listen.

Listen to the sound of **sh** in f**sh** and **sh**ip.
Listen again. Which words have a short **i** sound?

Make a list with your class.

Fix-It Fish

1 This fish can fix things.

I can fix this ship.

2 He is fixing a ship.

Can you fix it?
Yes, I can.

3 He is fixing a swing for the little fish.

Can you fix my wing, please?
Yes, I can. Just a minute.

4 He can fix fins and wings.

Thank you, Fix-it Fish!
You're welcome!

5 Goodbye!

4 Act out the story.

Make puppets and act out the story.

5 On the farm

> 5.6 The Little Red Hen

We are going to...
- read, talk about and act out a story.

Reading tip

Look at the pictures.

What is Little Red Hen making in this story?

Who is **not** helping her?

1 Listen and read.

The Little Red Hen

This folktale is told in many countries. It was probably first told in Russia.

1. I am making bread today.

2. Hello, Duck, Hello, Chick. Can you please help me pick the wheat?
Sorry, I'm busy.
Me too

3. I am picking the wheat myself.

5.6 Read and respond

4

Hello, Duck, Hello, Chick. Can you please help me grind the wheat?

Sorry, I'm busy.

Me too.

5

I am grinding the wheat myself.

6

Hello, Duck, Hello, Chick. Can you please help me make the bread?

Sorry, I'm busy.

Me too.

7

I am making the bread myself.

5 On the farm

8

Will you wash the dishes?

Will you sweep the floor?

Can we please eat your bread?

Yes, I will.

Yes, I will.

9

We're all eating the bread.

It's delicious!

10

Thank you, Chick. Thank you, Duck. You are very helpful.

You're welcome.

5.6 Read and respond

2 Story map: *The Little Red Hen*

Look at the story map and say what is happening.

Little Red Hen is picking the wheat.

3 Values: Helping others

Do Duck and Chick help Little Red Hen make the bread?

Read all the sentences where Hen has to do the work herself.

If Duck and Chick were helpful friends, what would they say when Hen asks, 'Can you help me?'

How do you help your friends? How do your friends help you?

4 Write your favourite ending.

At the end of this story, all the characters eat the bread.

In some other stories, Little Red Hen says to Duck and Chick, 'You did not help make the bread. So, now you cannot eat the bread.'

Which ending do you like best?

Draw a picture and add speech bubbles.
What does Little Hen say?

5 On the farm

> 5.7 Project challenge

Work with a partner or in a group to make the project.

Then share the project with your class.

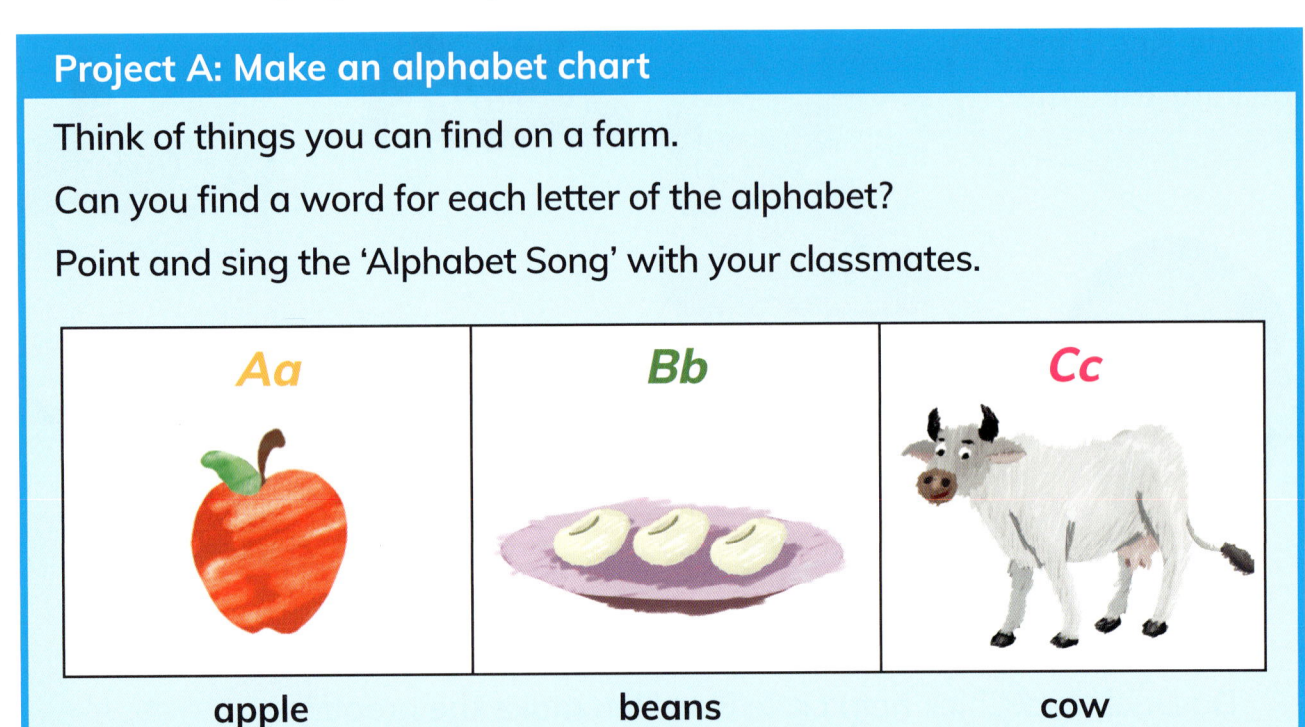

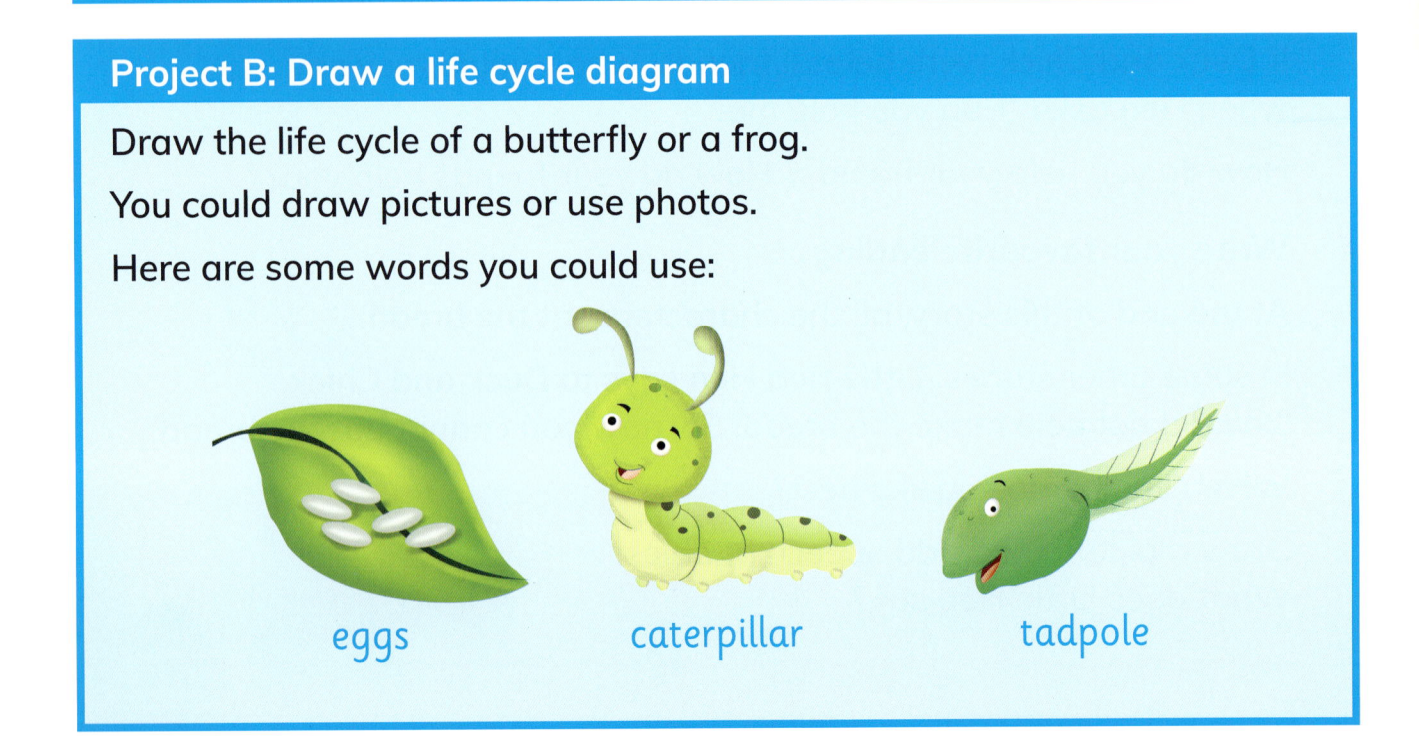

Project A: Make an alphabet chart

Think of things you can find on a farm.

Can you find a word for each letter of the alphabet?

Point and sing the 'Alphabet Song' with your classmates.

Aa	Bb	Cc
apple	beans	cow

Project B: Draw a life cycle diagram

Draw the life cycle of a butterfly or a frog.

You could draw pictures or use photos.

Here are some words you could use:

eggs   caterpillar   tadpole

5.7 Project challenge

Project C: Draw a picture of a farm

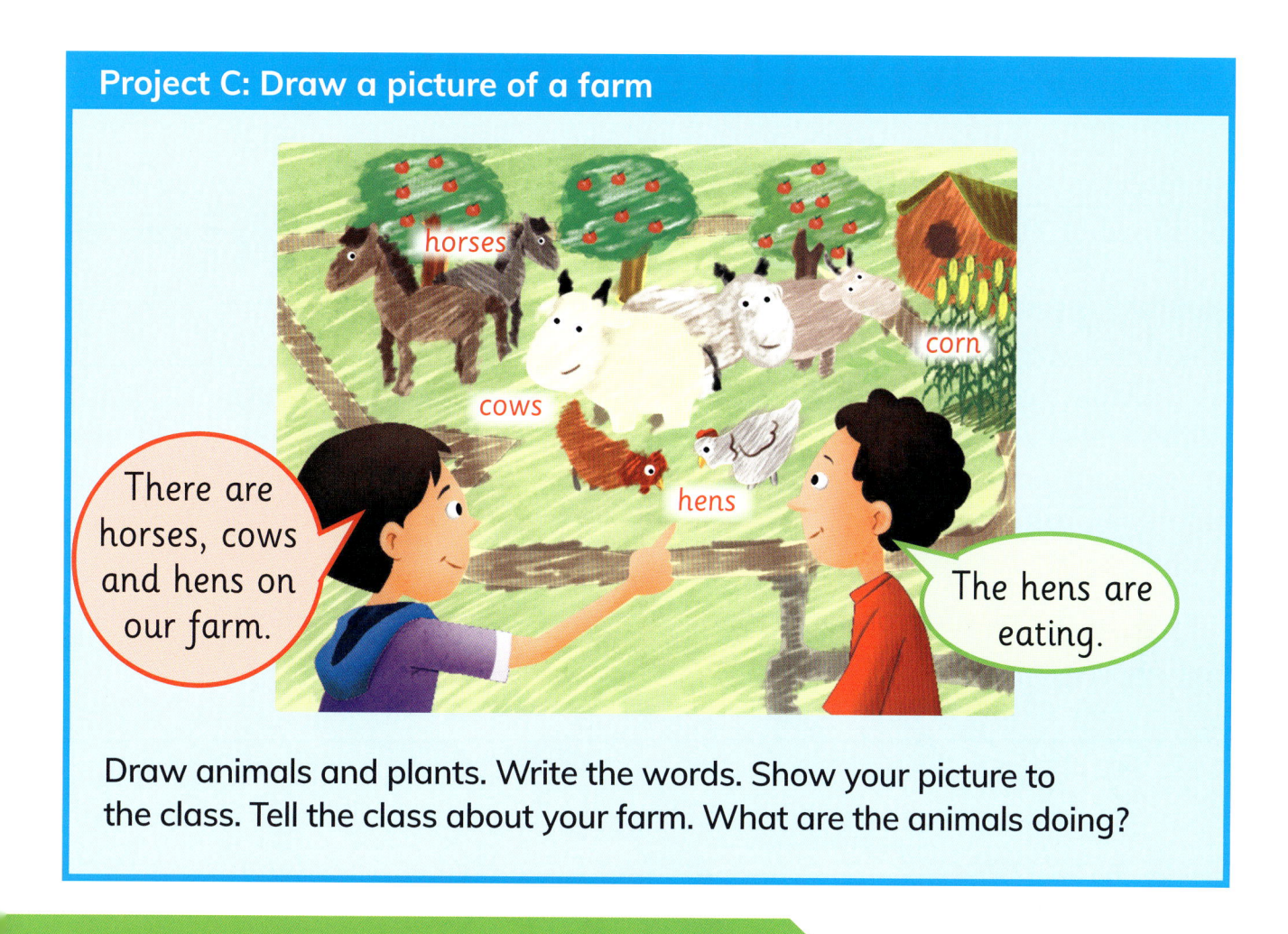

horses
corn
cows
hens

There are horses, cows and hens on our farm.

The hens are eating.

Draw animals and plants. Write the words. Show your picture to the class. Tell the class about your farm. What are the animals doing?

What part of the project did you like best?

Look what I can do!

I can name things on a farm.

I can talk about what people are doing.

I can learn about how plants and animals grow and change.

I can ask and answer questions.

I can read and write words with short i.

I can read, talk about and act out a story.

6 My five senses

> 6.1 How do we use our five senses?

We are going to...
- name our five senses.

Getting started

How do we use our senses?

Look at the picture for some ideas.

1 Listen and point.

Look at the things in the picture.

100

6.1 Think about it

2   Listen, point and say.

Listen to the sentence and say the missing word.

| see | hear | smell | taste | touch |

3   Look at the park.

Working in pairs, say what you can **see**, **hear**, **smell**, **touch** and **taste** in the park.

4   Read and listen.

Put the stickers on as you say the poem.
Point to your **eyes**, **ears**, **nose** and **mouth** as you say the words.

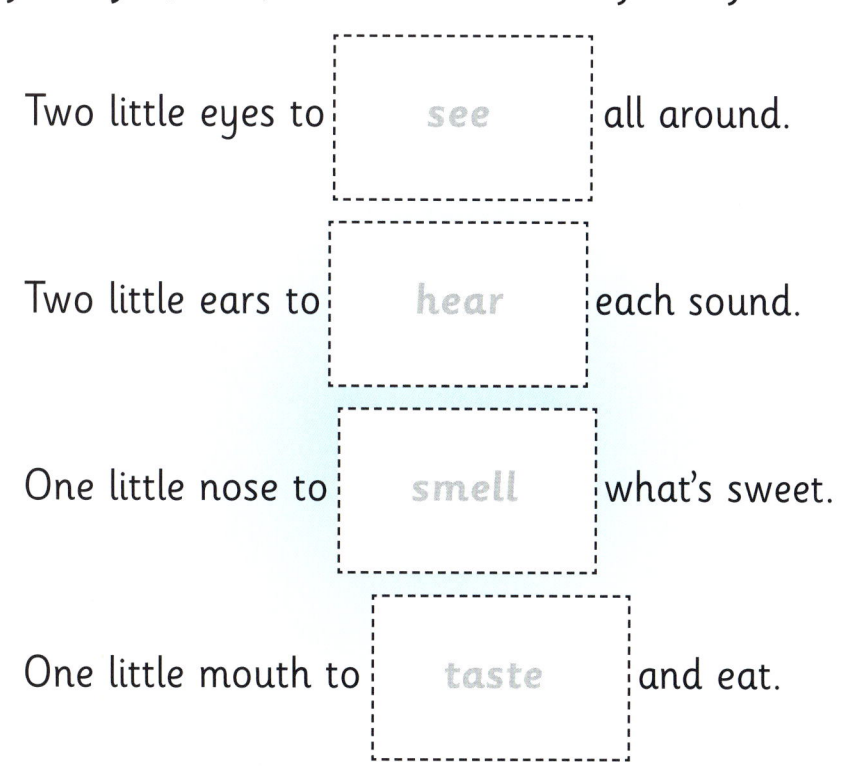

Two little eyes to *see* all around.

Two little ears to *hear* each sound.

One little nose to *smell* what's sweet.

One little mouth to *taste* and eat.

Watch this!

101

6 My five senses

> 6.2 What do you hear?

We are going to...
- talk about sounds.

1 Listen to the instruments.

Five musicians are playing in the park.
Point to each instrument as you listen to the sound.

piano violin drum saxophone triangle

2 Sing the song.

Pretend you are playing each instrument.

The Music Man

I am the music man.
I come from down your way
And I can play!
What can you play?
I can play the **piano**,
the **piano**, the **piano**.
I can play the **piano**, **pia-piano**.

6.2 Let's explore

3 Guess the instrument.

Pretend to play an instrument. Can your friends guess what you are playing?

Are you playing the piano?

Are you playing the bass drum?

No, I'm not.

Yes, I am

4 Experiment with drums.

You will need 3 drums.
- The first drum is a pot made of metal.
- The second drum is a box made of cardboard.
- The third drum is made of plastic.

a Play the first and second drums. Which is louder?
b Play the first and third drums. Which is louder?
c Which drum makes your favourite sound?

5 Write about your favourite sound.

What's your favourite sound?
Is it the sound of rain? A favourite song?
Your mum saying 'Hello!'?
Is it the sound of a flute or guitar?

Brainstorm ideas with your class. Then draw a picture and write a sentence:

My favourite sound is _____.

6 My five senses

> 6.3 Using your five senses

We are going to...
- describe and compare things.

1 What is different?

Work with a partner. Find 5 things that are different in Picture A and B.

Picture A

a   There is 1 boy and 2 _____.
b   There are no teachers.
c   There are _____ drums.
d   The boy is playing the _____.
e   _____

Picture B

a   There is 1 boy and 1 _____.
b   There is a _____ playing the saxophone.
c   There are _____ drums.
d   The boy is playing the _____.
e   _____

2 Talk about smells!

Work in pairs to talk about smells.

Do you like the smell of onion?

Yes, I do.

No, I don't.

onion    fish    soap    mango    flowers    smoke

3 What does it feel like?

Imagine you're in bed. It's dark. Your hand touches something soft. Is it your teddy bear or your book?

Key word

imagine

We can learn a lot about an object by touching. We can tell if it is:

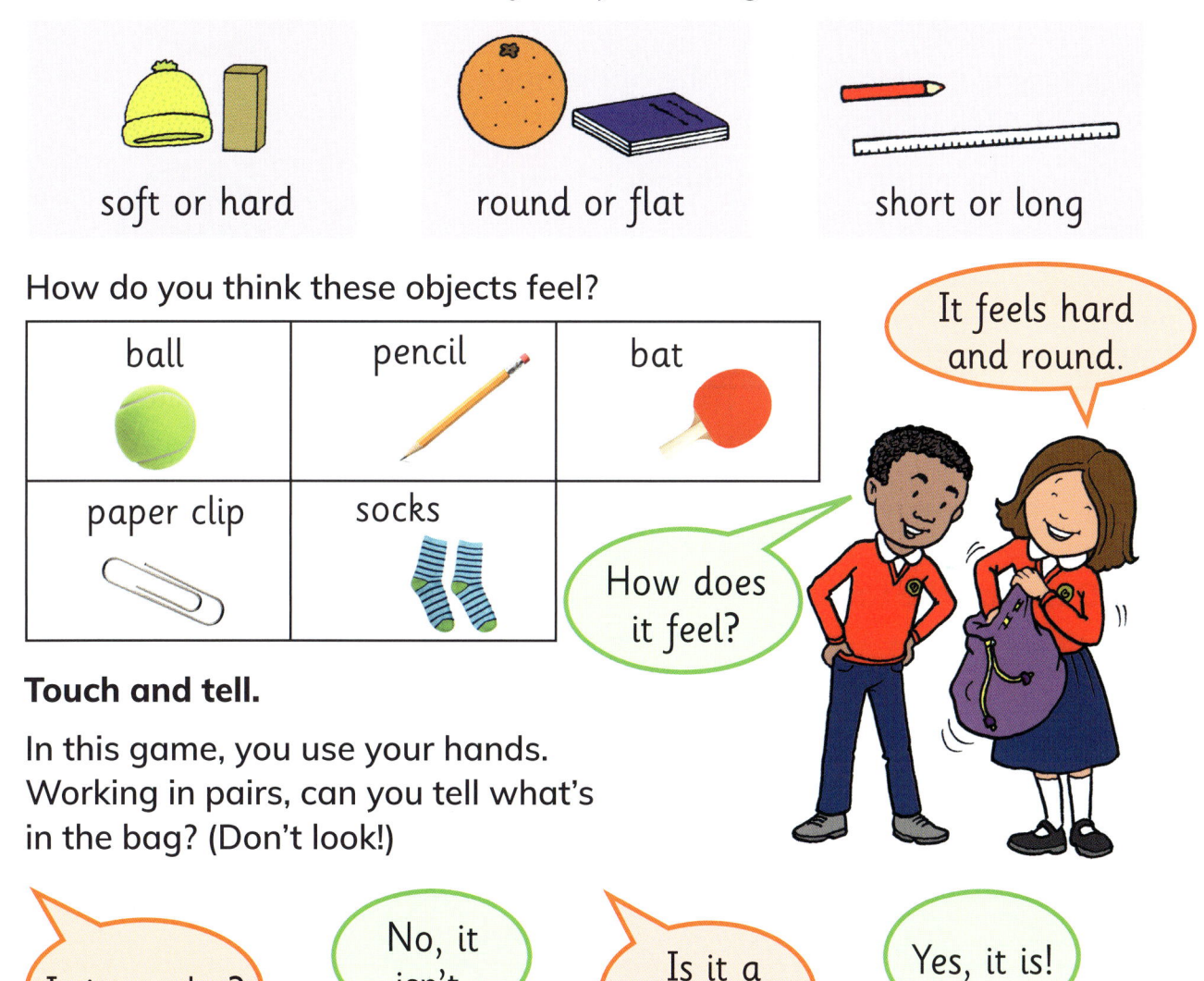

soft or hard   round or flat   short or long

How do you think these objects feel?

ball	pencil	bat
paper clip	socks	

It feels hard and round.

How does it feel?

4 Touch and tell.

In this game, you use your hands. Working in pairs, can you tell what's in the bag? (Don't look!)

Is it a ruler?

No, it isn't.

Is it a pencil?

Yes, it is!

5 Listen and tell.

In this game, you use your ears. What's in the box? Working with a partner, shake, listen and tell.

6 My five senses

> 6.4 Sweet and loud

We are going to...
- use our senses to describe things.

1 **Describe the colours.**

Imagine a red apple. Cut the apple open. What colour do you see inside?

Read the clues and find the matching fruits.

a   It's red outside and white inside.

b   It's yellow outside and white inside.

c   It's green outside and pink inside.

d   It's brown outside and green inside.

e   It's orange outside and orange inside.

outside
inside

apple
banana
watermelon
kiwi
orange

2 **Describe the tastes.**

lemon   banana   strawberry   carrot   mango   bean

Sweet	Not sweet	Juicy	Not juicy
	lemon	lemon	

a   How do these fruits and vegetables taste? Are they sweet or not sweet? Write your answers on a chart.

b   Sort the same fruits and vegetables in a different way. This time ask, 'Are they juicy or not juicy?'

Write your answers on a chart.

A lemon is not sweet!

6.4 Use of English

3   Sing the song.

Sing the song. Then make your own verse, singing about different fruits.

> **Strawberries** are lovely and sweet
> They're my favourite fruit to eat.
> Juicy **mangos** are so yummy.
> 'Thank you, thank you!' says my tummy.
> **Bananas** and **kiwis**; **oranges** too.
> Fruit is yummy and good for you!

4   What sounds can you hear?

Listen to a guitar.

- It can make **loud** sounds and **quiet** sounds.
- It can make **high** sounds and **low** sounds.

Listen and say if the sounds are loud or quiet, high or low.

5   Make a rubber-band guitar.

Use a small open box or container and a rubber band.

Pluck the rubber band to make a sound. Hold the rubber band with your fingers and pluck again. Is the sound different or the same?

- Can you make a **loud** sound?
- Can you make a **quiet** sound?
- Can you make a **high** sound?
- Can you make a **low** sound?

6   Make musical glasses.

Pour different amounts of water in 3 tall drinking glasses.

Tap each glass with a spoon. Which glass makes a **high** sound?
Which glass makes a **low** sound? Play some music!

107

6 My five senses

> 6.5 Short o

We are going to...

- read and write words with a short o.

b**o**x

on

fr**o**g

1 Listen, look and say.

Listen to the short o sound.
Say the words.
Use the words to make a sentence.

2 Which picture?

Match the picture to the sentence.

a   The frog is on a log.   b   The fox is on a rock.   c   The fox is hot.

1   2   3

3 Listen to the rhyme.

Say it and act it out.

> You put the oil in the pot,
> And you let it get hot.
> You put the popcorn in,
> And you start to grin.
> Sizzle, sizzle, sizzle, sizzle,
> Pop, pop, pop!

Which words in this poem have the short o sound?

6.5 Letters and sounds

4 **Read and listen.**

Say the words that have the short **o** sound. Then act out the story!

Tick, tock, hop!

1 Hi. My name is Bob.

Bob the frog hops to the pond.
Hop, hop, stop. Hop, hop, stop.

2 Hi, Fred. What's that?

It's a clock.

Bob hears an odd sound.
Tick, tock. Tick, tock.
He sees his friend Fred, the fox.

3 I like that sound!

Fred hits a rock with two sticks.
Tap-tap, bop! Tap-tap, bop!

4 We like that sound!

The fish in the pond hear the sound.
Flip, flop. Flip, flop.

5 Come on, Bob! You can hop too.

Two rabbits hear the sound.
Hop, hop, hop! Hop, hop, hop!

6

Tick, tock.
Hop, hop, hop! We can dance to the sound of the clock!

5 **Put your stickers in your Picture dictionary: log, rock, pond, stick.**
On which page do the stickers belong? Find the correct page.

6 My five senses

> 6.6 Five Friends and the Elephant

We are going to...

- read, talk about and act out a story.

1 Listen and read.

Five Friends and the Elephant

This story is from India.

1 A man arrives with an elephant. It's the first elephant to visit this land!

Five blind friends want to meet it. They can't see, but they can use their other senses to learn about the world.

2 The five friends go to meet the elephant.

"Can we meet your elephant, please?"

"Of course. My elephant is tame and gentle."

3 The first friend feels the elephant's long, thin tail.

"The elephant feels like a rope!"

Stop and talk.
What do you think the next friend will do and say?

6.6 Read and respond

4 The second friend feels the elephant's side.

This elephant feels like a wall!

5 The third friend feels the elephant's leg.

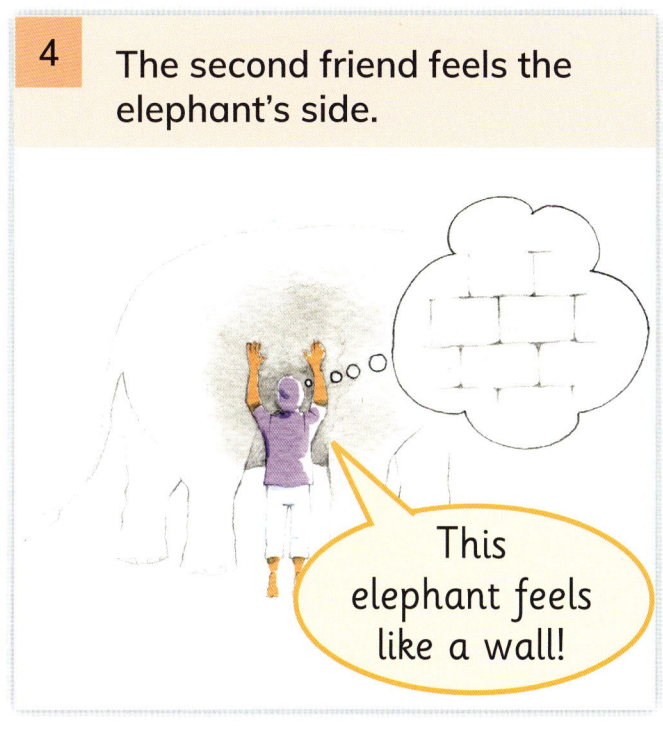

This elephant feels like a big strong tree!

6 The fourth friend feels the elephant's ear.

This elephant feels like a giant fan!

7 The fifth friend feels the elephant's trunk.

This elephant feels like a long wiggly snake!

111

6   My five senses

8

All of you are right, my friends. My elephant has many different parts and each part feels different.

Why don't you help me take care of my elephant? You can get to know the whole elephant better.

9

The elephant smells like a horse.

The elephant likes the taste of apples.

The elephant has a loud voice.

We like this elephant!

So the five friends help the man take care of the elephant.
They learn many interesting things!

6.6 Read and respond

2 Discuss the story.

Why do the five friends need to touch the elephant?

3 Explore parts of the elephant.

Which part of the elephant feels like a...

wall   rope
snake   tree
giant fan

4 Act it out!

Make a paper elephant or use a toy elephant. Touch the different parts of the elephant as you act out the story.

5 Values: Everyone is included.

Children who can see and children who can't see like to play together. Here are two special toys that are fun for everyone.

a   This ball makes a buzzing sound. How can children who cannot see catch this ball?

b   You can play games using this dice with raised dots. How can children who cannot see count the number of dots?

6 Write and draw.

Imagine that the five friends meet a gentle deer. Each friend touches a different part of the deer and says how it feels. What does each friend say?

Write speech bubbles for the five friends.

| long | thin | soft | hard | furry | wiggly |

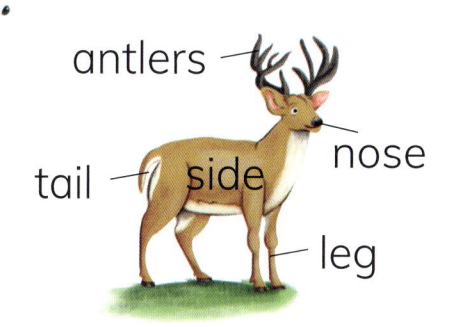

Its nose feels soft.

113

6 My five senses

> 6.7 Project challenge

Work with a partner or in a group to make the project.
Then share the project with your class.

Project A: Make a chart

Choose a question:
Do you like this smell?
or **Do you like this sound?**

Write the question on the chart. Draw 2 things you can smell or hear.

Do you like this smell?		Ian	Dora	Sofia		
	Yes, I do.	✔				
	No, I don't.					
	Yes, I do.					
	No, I don't.	✔				

Ask six friends the question. Mark their answers on the chart.

Project B: Make a book: Our favourite things

Write about your favourite things to see, hear, smell, taste and touch. Draw pictures, or copy and paste photos, of two things on each page.

Make a cover for your book. Write the title of the book and your names.

Share the book with your class.

page 1 Here are our favourite things to **see**.
page 2 Here are our favourite things to **hear**.
page 3 Here are our favourite things to **smell**.
page 4 Here are our favourite things to **taste**.
page 5 Here are our favourite things to **touch**.

6.7 Project challenge

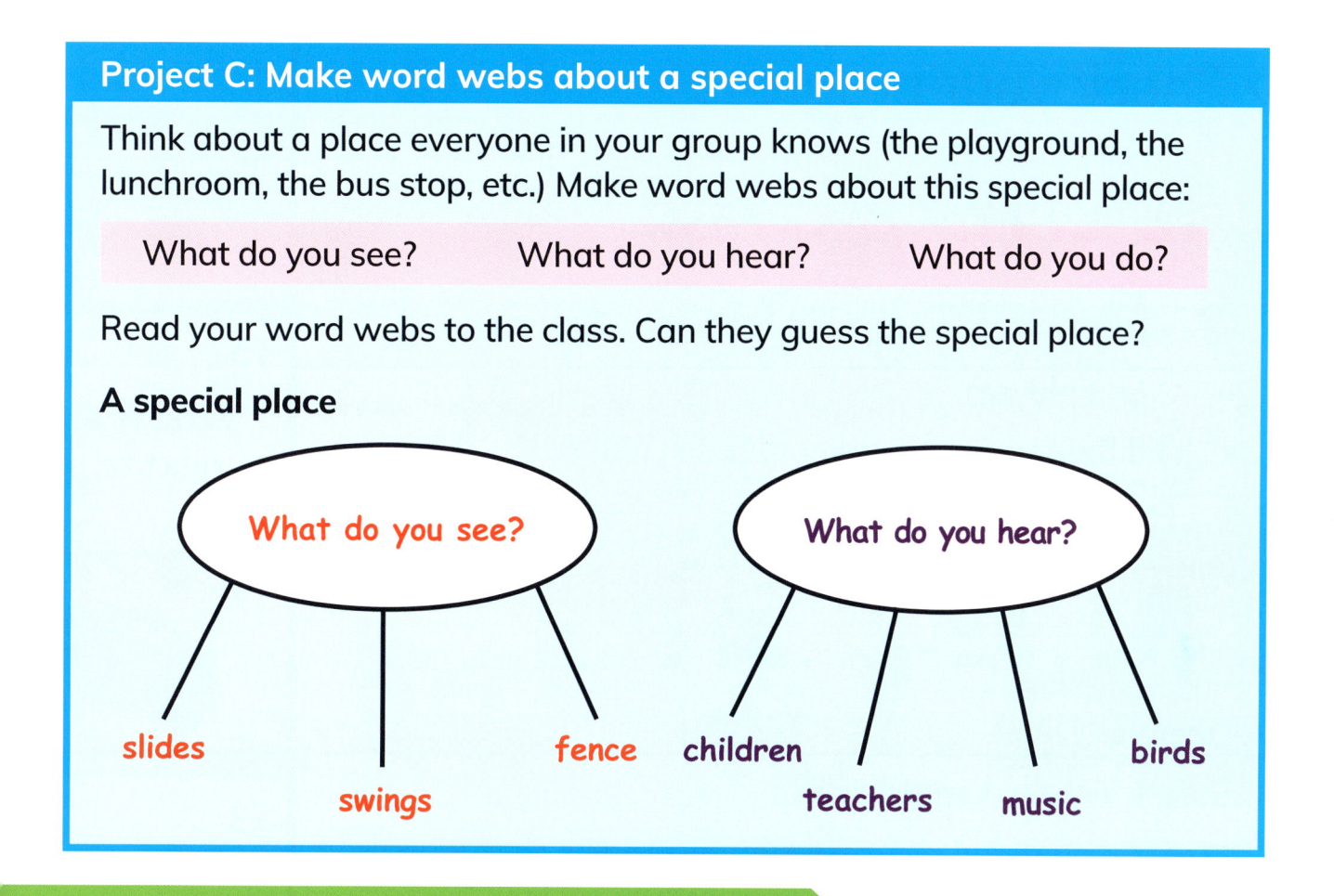

Project C: Make word webs about a special place

Think about a place everyone in your group knows (the playground, the lunchroom, the bus stop, etc.) Make word webs about this special place:

What do you see?   What do you hear?   What do you do?

Read your word webs to the class. Can they guess the special place?

A special place

What do you see?
- slides
- swings
- fence

What do you hear?
- children
- teachers
- music
- birds

What part of the project was the hardest?

Look what I can do!

I can name my five senses.
I can talk about sounds.
I can use my senses to describe and compare things.
I can read and write words with a short **o**.
I can listen to, read and act out a story.

6   Units 4–6: Review

> Check your progress

At the pond

You need:
- 2 to 3 players
- a different game marker for each player
- number cards.

Directions

Step 1. Take a number card.

Step 2. Count and move your game marker on the game track. Then do one of these things:
- Read the **word** or the **clue**. Go to the matching picture.
- Look at the picture. Say the word.
- Read and answer the **questions**.

Step 3. The first player to get to the pond is the winner!

16 It is tall.

15 Who is sitting next to you?

14

13 Take another turn!

12 rock

START

1

2 It has soft ears.

3 How many children are playing this game?

| 17 fish | 18 | 19 log | 20 bridge |

11	10 What is your teacher doing?	9 It is green.
		8 Cows eat this.
4 fox	5	6	7 What are you wearing?

117

7 Let's go!

> 7.1 How do we travel around?

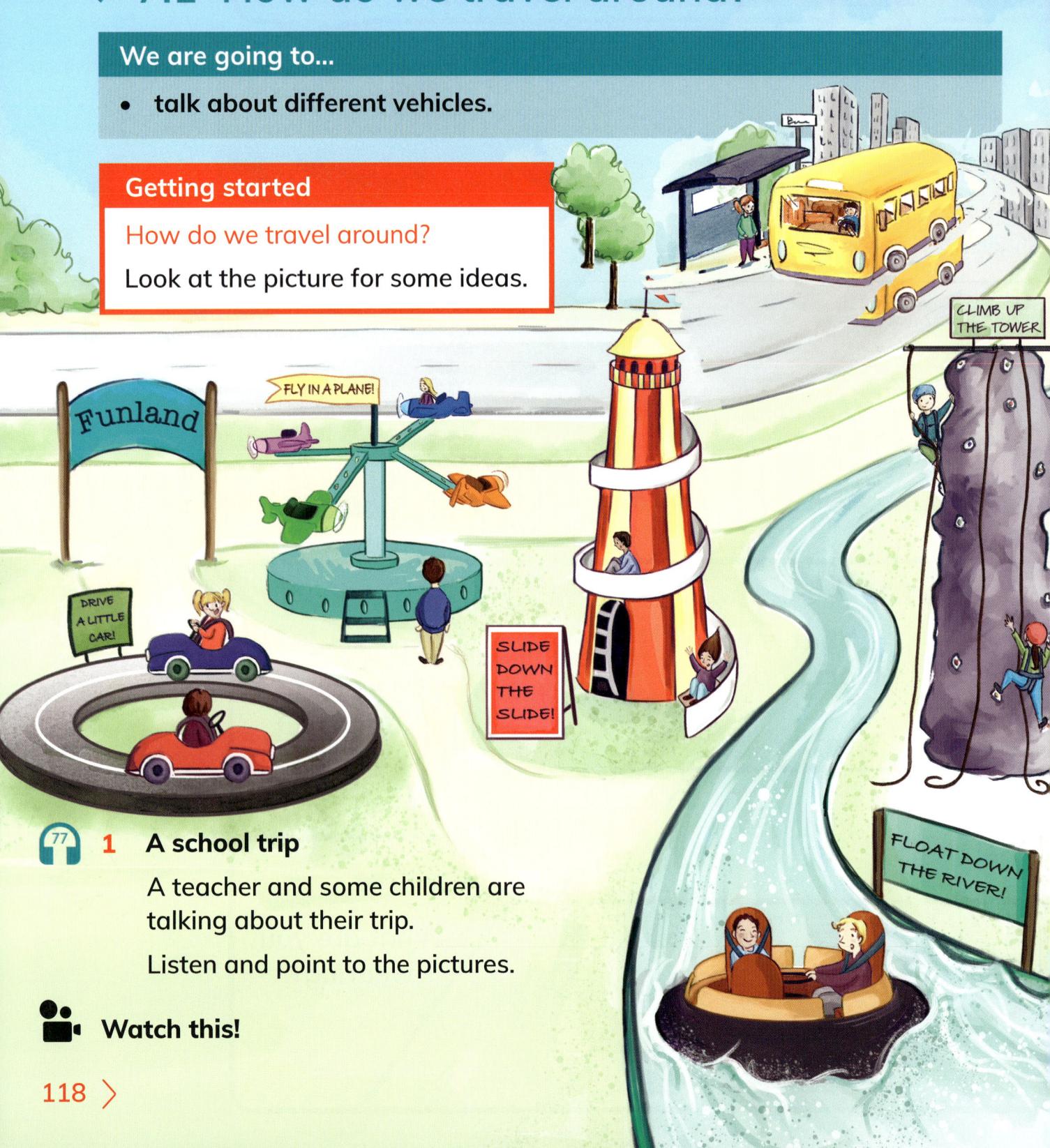

We are going to...
- talk about different vehicles.

Getting started
How do we travel around?
Look at the picture for some ideas.

FLY IN A PLANE!

Funland

DRIVE A LITTLE CAR!

SLIDE DOWN THE SLIDE!

CLIMB UP THE TOWER

FLOAT DOWN THE RIVER!

🎧 77 **1 A school trip**

A teacher and some children are talking about their trip.

Listen and point to the pictures.

🎥 **Watch this!**

118

7.1 Think about it

2 Listen, point and say.

Listen to the sentences and say the missing word.

climb   slide   float   drive   fly

3 Listen and write the letters.

What word do they spell?

4 Find it.

Tell your partner to find something in the picture.

Find something you can climb.

5 Read and listen.

Put the stickers on as you say the poem.
Act it out!

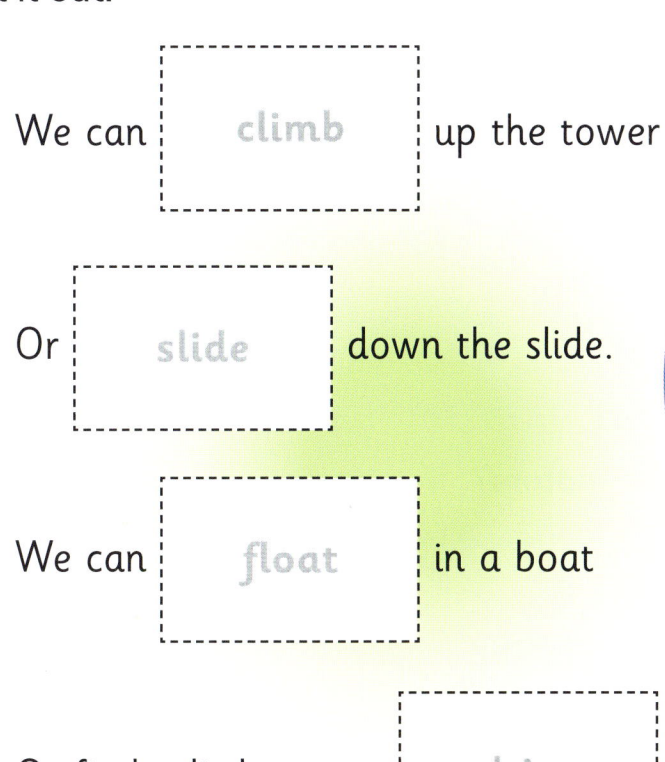

We can [climb] up the tower

Or [slide] down the slide.

We can [float] in a boat

Or find a little car to [drive].

119

7 Let's go!

7.2 Vehicles

We are going to...
- talk about different vehicles.

1 Take a ride in a snowmobile.

Point to the images as you listen and read.

In Alaska there is lots of snow in winter. You can ride a snowmobile.

Snowmobiles have skis instead of wheels, and the driver sits in the front.

They also have motors, which are very noisy.

Many Alaskan children ride a snowmobile to get to school in winter.

In spring, summer and autumn, children ride in a taxi, a seaplane or in a boat.

2 Talk about travelling.

Ask your partner:
- Does a bus have a motor?
- Does a boat have a motor?
- What other vehicles have motors?

Do you have to cross a bridge to get to school?

7.2 Let's explore

3 Sort the vehicles.

Sort these vehicles into groups.

It has wheels.	It doesn't have wheels.
A _____ has wheels.	A _____ doesn't have wheels.

bus   boat   train

snowmobile   plane   motorcycle

4 Sing the song!

Sing and do the actions.

The wheels on the bus

The wheels on the bus go round and round,
round and round, round and round.
The wheels on the bus go round and round,
All day long.

swish! — wipers
clink! — money 
chatter — children 
'shhhh!' — driver 
DING! — bell 

5 Draw and write.

Draw a picture of a bus. Write words to label these things:

wheels   windows   door   driver   wipers

121

7 Let's go!

> 7.3 Make a helicopter and a plane

We are going to...

- follow instructions.

1 Make a helicopter.
- Take some paper.
- Cut out a helicopter shape.
- Fold it.
- Attach the paper clip.
- Fly your helicopter.

122

7.3 Science

2 Helicopter experiment

Work with a partner.

Drop your helicopters at the same time.

Which helicopter stays up longer?

3 Make a plane.

- Choose your favourite colour paper.
- Fold the piece of paper down the middle.
- Fold the top corners down to the middle.
- Fold the left wing back. Fold the right wing back.
- Fly your paper plane.

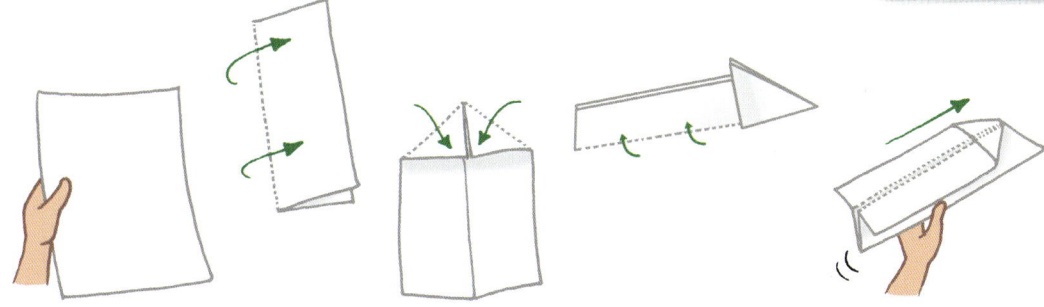

Key word

fold

4 Plane experiment

Stand side by side. Throw your planes!

Which plane flies further?

5 Write about it.

Write the name of the winners, like this:

Marco's helicopter stayed up longer.

Ting's plane flew further.

123

7 Let's go!

7.4 Describing things

We are going to...
- describe things using size, colour and number.

1 Sing a song.

Point to the image as you sing.

My big blue boat

Come for a ride in my big blue boat,
My big blue boat, my big blue boat.
Come for a ride in my big blue boat,
Out on the deep blue sea.

My big blue boat has two red sails,
Two red sails, two red sails.
My big blue boat has two red sails,
Out on the deep blue sea.

Language detective

Look at the title of the song. Which word comes first – the **colour** word or the **size** word?

2 Draw a sailing boat.

You need some crayons. Tell your partner how to draw a sailing boat. Choose colours you like.

Draw a big **green** triangle.

Draw a **blue** line down the middle.

Draw a long **red** rectangle.

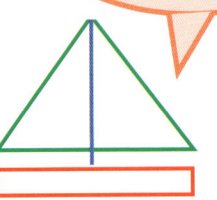

Find 1 blue snowmobile.

Find 2 yellow buses.

3 **Play a look and find game.**

Read the two clues. Look at the picture.
Write two more clues.

Put all the clues in a bag. Take turns choosing
a clue and reading it to the class.

Find 3 red cars.

4 **Make a mural with your class.**

Make different coloured buses, cars and motorcycles.
Park them in the car park. Count them.

Write some sentences about your mural.

There are 3 green buses.   There are 2 red cars.

125

7 Let's go!

> 7.5 Long e spelling ee

We are going to…

- read and write words with the long e spelling ee.

1 Listen, look and say.

Listen to the long e sound. Say the words.

a   Which two letters make the long e sound in these words?

b   Which two words rhyme?

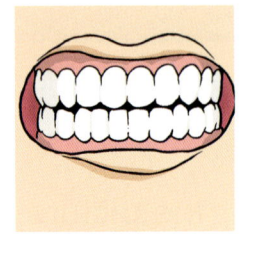

tree   teeth   knee

c   Add **ee** to make the name of part of a bicycle:

wh __ __ l

2 Words that start with wh

The word wheel begins with **wh**.
Many question words also begin with **wh**.

How many more can you think of?

When?   Why?   Wh____?   Wh____?   Wh____?

3 What's in the picture?

Working in pairs, find things that make a long **e** sound.

4 Questions and answers

Match the questions and answers.

What do bees make?   A Jeep goes BEEP BEEP.

Where do sheep sleep?   Bees make honey.

What sound does a Jeep make?   Sheep sleep in a field.

5 Put stickers in your Picture dictionary: sheep, deer, bee.

On which page do the stickers belong? Find the correct page.

6 Read and listen.

Which words do you hear with the long **e** sound?

Please keep out!

7 Make a 'keep out' sign.

You could put it on your bedroom door!

7 Let's go!

> 7.6 Travelling around

We are going to...

- read and write about different vehicles.

1 **Before you read**

This text has 3 sections.

Each section starts with a heading that is written in blue letters.

Read the headings, then look at the photos.

What do you think each section is about?

2 **Listen and read.**

Travelling around

On land, on water, under the ground

There are many kinds of vehicles. Some travel on land. Some travel on water. Some travel under the ground.

You can travel on land in a **tractor**.
A tractor moves slowly.

You can travel on the water in a **hydrofoil**.
The ride is fast and bumpy!

You can travel under the city in an **underground train**.

It's a good way to get around in a city.

128

7.6 Read and respond

How many wheels?

Vehicles have different numbers of wheels.
Bicycles have two wheels.
Tricycles have three wheels.
Unicycles have one wheel.

Some **trucks** have four wheels.
Other trucks have many wheels.
How many wheels are on the big white truck?

Most **wheelchairs** have two big wheels and two little wheels.
Special wheelchairs for races have three wheels.
They go very fast.

129

7 Let's go!

Just for fun

It's fun to move around in different ways.
You can ride a **skateboard** in a park. You can jump over things.
You can put on **skis** and ski down a snowy mountain.
Do you like rolling down a hill? Climb inside a **zorb**!
A zorb is a very big ball. You roll down the hill very fast.

7.6 Read and respond

3 Many kinds of vehicles

Work with a partner. Can you name all the vehicles?
Which one is biggest? Which one is fastest? Which one is most exciting?

4 Make a chart.

Look at the vehicles again. Which ones are powered by people?
Which ones are powered by a motor?

Can you think of any more vehicles to add to the chart?

People-powered vehicles	Motor-powered vehicles
skateboard	underground train

5 Values: stay safe!

When we travel, we must remember to stay safe.
Match each picture to the safety rule.

Stay safe on your **bike**. Wear a helmet!

Stay safe on the **Underground**.
Stay behind the yellow line.

Stay safe in your **car**. Wear a seat belt!

6 Creative writing: My favourite way to travel

Do you like travelling in a train or a plane?
On a motorbike or a boat? Where do you like to go?

Draw a picture and write some sentences.

> I like travelling in a train.
> I go to my grandma's house by train.

131

7 Let's go!

> 7.7 Project challenge

Work with a partner or in a group to make the project.
Then share the project with your class.

Project A: Do a travel survey

Work in pairs and choose 3 vehicles. Make a survey chart.

		Jack	Zhou	Bibi
Bus	Yes, I do.		✔	
	No, I don't.	✔		
Train	Yes, I do.		✔	
	No, I don't.	✔		
Car	Yes, I do.	✔	✔	
	No, I don't.			

When your survey is finished, talk about your chart.

How many children think travelling by bus is fun?

How many children think travelling by bus isn't fun?

Project B: Make a word flip book

Make a book like this.

Write these letters on the short left-hand pages: **b, s, tr, kn, thr**

Write these letters on the long right-hand pages: **ee**

On each left-hand page, draw a picture of the word you make.

7.7 Project challenge

Project C: Make up new verses for a poem

Read this poem about a plane.

> Little silver plane
> Up in the sky,
> Where are you going to
> Flying so high?
>
> Over the mountains
> Over the sea
> Little silver plane
> Please take me.

Write new verses of the poem about your favourite flying machines:

a **jet**   a **helicopter**   a **balloon**   a **kite**

What size is your flying machine?
Is it **big** or **little**? Is it **giant** (very big) or **tiny** (very little)?
What colour is it?

Change the words in green. Write at least 2 new verses for the poem.

You can draw pictures or find photos on the computer of the flying machines in your poem.

Or you can build models of your flying machines.

What is something new that you learned from this project?

Look what I can do!

	😐	🙂
I can talk about different vehicles.	○	○
I can follow instructions.	○	○
I can describe things using size, colour and number.	○	○
I can read and write words with the long e spelling ee.	○	○
I can read and write about different vehicles.	○	○

8 ▶ City places

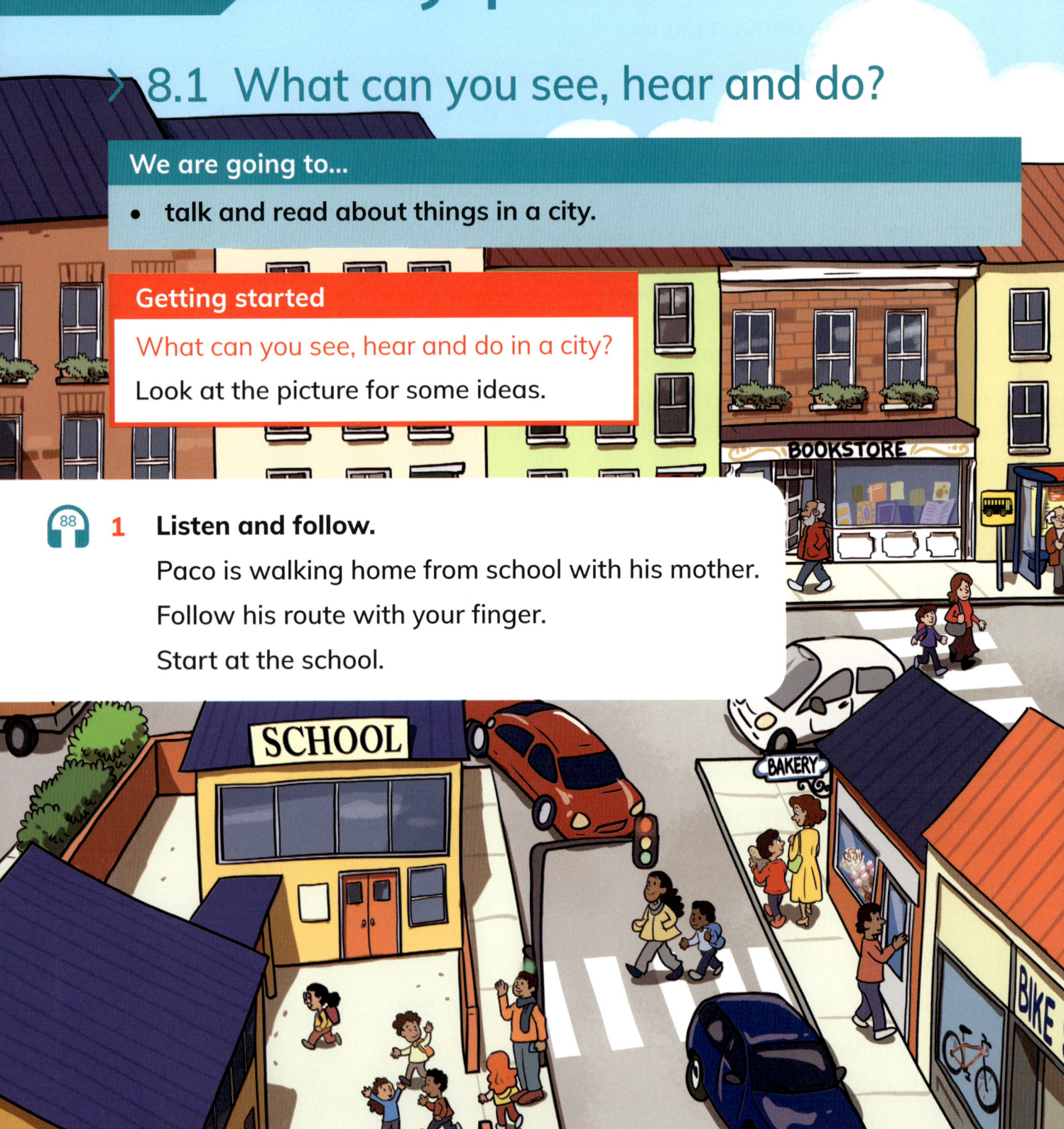

▶ 8.1 What can you see, hear and do?

We are going to...
- talk and read about things in a city.

Getting started

What can you see, hear and do in a city?
Look at the picture for some ideas.

🎧 88 **1 Listen and follow.**

Paco is walking home from school with his mother.
Follow his route with your finger.
Start at the school.

8.1 Think about it

2 **Listen, point and say.**

road   pavement   shops   traffic   traffic light   bus stop

Listen again and clap the syllables.

How many syllables are there in each word or phrase?

3 **Answer the questions.**
   a How many shops do you see?
   b What can you buy in the shops?
   c When the traffic light is red, what should the cars do?

4 **Read and listen.**

Put the stickers on as you say the poem.

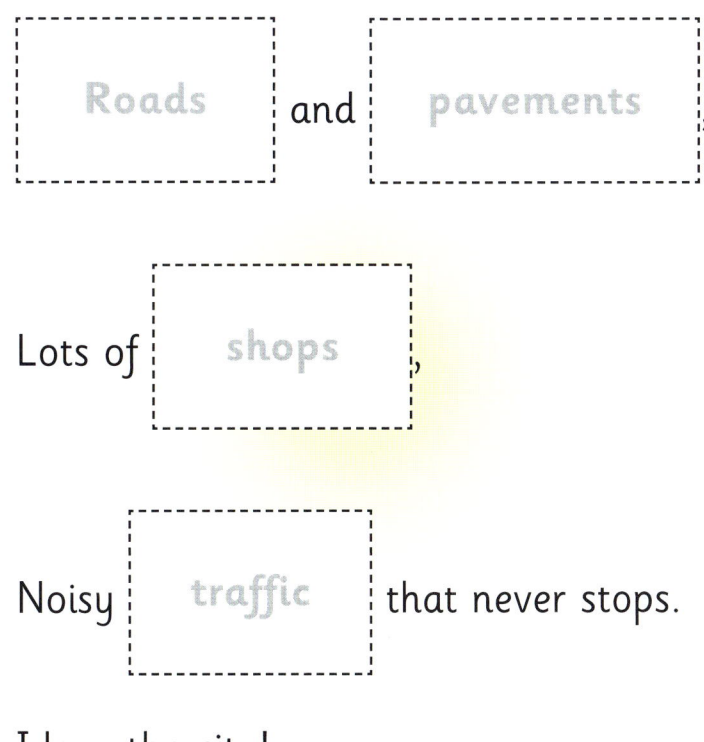

Roads and pavements,

Lots of shops,

Noisy traffic that never stops.

I love the city!

Watch this!

8 City places

8.2 Around the city

We are going to...
- talk and read about things in a city.

1 Point and say.

It's important to watch the traffic light when you cross the road! Make a traffic light.

Point to the lights as you say and listen to the poem.

The Traffic Light
Red means STOP.
Green means GO.
Yellow means WAIT,
Even if you're late.

2 Play the game 'Traffic lights'.

Listen to your teacher: green light is walk forward, red light is stop!

3 Write and draw.

Think of a city or town that you know.
What can you **hear** in that city?
What can you **see** in that city?
Brainstorm ideas with your class.
Write two sentences and draw a picture.

Writing tip

Look at Picture dictionary page 175 for ideas.

In __Barcelona__, I can hear __motorcycles__ and __boats__.
I can see __pavements__ and __shops__.

8.2 Let's explore

4 **What colour is the next door?**

The **first** house has a red door. The **second** house has a yellow door. The **third** house has a red door.

Talk with your partner. What colour doors do the **fourth**, **fifth** and **sixth** houses have? What is the colour **pattern**?

The builders are putting new doors on the last four houses.

Follow the colour pattern and colour the **seventh**, **eighth**, **ninth** and **tenth** houses.

Ask your partner questions:

*What colour is the door on the **eighth** house?*

5 **City flowers**

Look at the new flower garden!
The men are planting the flowers in a colour pattern.

Work in pairs and talk about the colour pattern with your partner. Colour the rest of the flowers to continue the pattern.

Ask your partner questions:

*What colour is the **ninth** flower?*

8 City places

8.3 City living

We are going to...
- talk and read about things in a city.

1 Before you read

Look at the photos. What do you see?
Can you find these things where you live?

2 Listen and read.

I like living in a city

I live in a city.

It's a great place to live.

There are tall buildings and short buildings.

Some buildings have gardens on top!

There's a park in my city.

It's very pretty. It has flowers,

a pond, and an ice-cream seller!

I like eating ice-cream in the park.

Sometimes parks and cities get dirty.

We all need to keep our city clean.

Don't forget to put your litter in a bin!

8.3 Global awareness

3 Where do you live?

Do you live in a city or the country? Is there a park near you? What other places are near your home?

a park   a bakery   a library   a zoo

There's a park near my home.

4 Ask and answer.

Ask your partner questions.

Where can I ...

buy bread?   see an elephant?   play on a slide?

*Where can I read **a book**?*

*Go to the **library**.*

5 Put stickers in your Picture dictionary:
library, bakery, park, zoo.

On which page do the stickers belong? Find the correct page.

6 Can I have an ice-cream?

Listen. Then practise with a partner.

Choose a flavour. Choose a size.

Key word

choose

Hi! Can I have an ice-cream, please?

Sure! What flavour?

A **banana** ice-cream, please.

Big or small?

Big!

Here you are.

Thank you!

139

8 City places

8.4 This or these?

We are going to...
- describe and ask questions using **this**, **that** and **these**.

1 Talk about the towns.

Look at the town on the table.

Look at the town on the map.

Listen to the children talk about the two towns. Point to the things they talk about.

This town has a library.

That town has a bakery.

2 Act it out.

Listen to the conversation again. Can you fill in the missing words?

Then practise the conversation with your partner.

Point to the places in the picture.

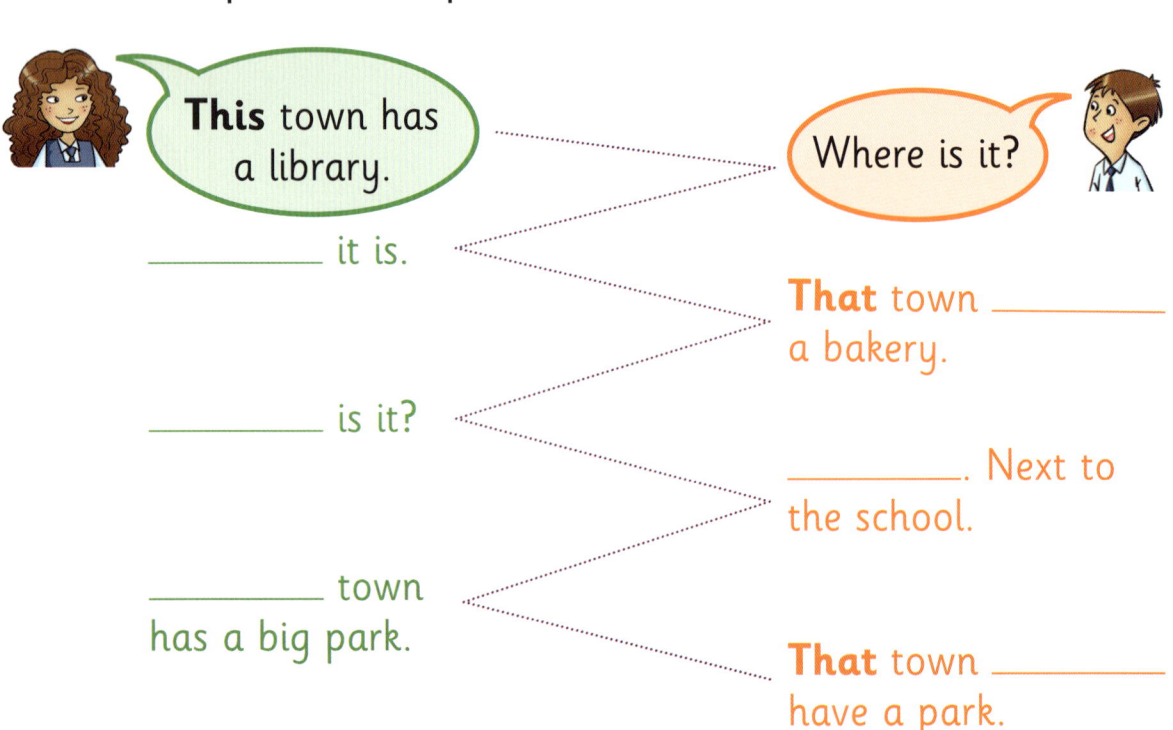

This town has a library.

_____ it is.

_____ is it?

_____ town has a big park.

Where is it?

That town _____ a bakery.

_____. Next to the school.

That town _____ have a park.

8.4 Use of English

3   Sing a city song.

Listen to the song. Join in! Can you find the word **this** in the song?

> **My city**
>
> This is my city,
> Come along with me.
> The park is so pretty,
> We can stop and have our tea.
>
> We can climb a tall tower,
> There's such a lot to see!
> This is my city,
> A place for you and me!

4   Play a game: What is this? What are these?

You need 2 players and 8 counters.

a   Player 1 points to a picture and asks a question.

   What is this? or **What are these?**

b   Player 2 says the word and puts a counter on the picture.
     or Player 2 says, **I don't know**.

c   Play until all the pictures have a counter.

Language detective

When do you say **this**?

When do you say **these**?

141

8 City places

> 8.5 –y endings

We are going to...
- read and write words that end in –y
- name opposites.

1 Listen, say and clap.

Clap the syllables of the words: my city.

a How many syllables are there in my?

b How many syllables are there in city?

> The –y sounds like the long i.

2 Different sounds of –y

The words my and city both end with –y, but the –y has a different sound.

> The –y sounds like the long e.

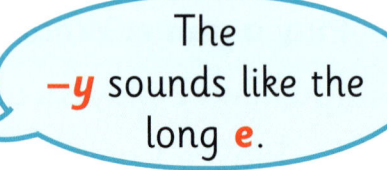

Words with 1 syllable	Words with 2 syllables (or more)
my try	city pretty
The -y sounds like the long i.	The -y sounds like the long e.

Say each word. Clap and count the syllables. What sound does –y have?

baby    cry    fly    carry    happy   sky

3 Which –y word?

Work with a partner. Use a word above to finish each sentence.

a The _____ is blue today.

b I _____ when I am sad.

c I can _____ my teddy bears.

d Look! I can _____!

e A _____ is very small.

f I'm not sad. I'm _____!

8.5 Letters and sounds

4 Opposites

These words are opposites:

dirty   clean   noisy   quiet

What is the opposite of **big**?

5 Read the poem.

a Work with a partner and say the words that are missing. Then listen to check.

b Match the pair of photos to a sentence in the poem.

Opposites

The opposite of **yes** is **no**.
The opposite of **stop** is _____.
The opposite of **good** is **bad**.
The opposite of **happy** is _____.

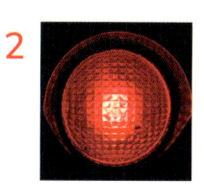

The opposite of **hot** is **cold**.
The opposite of **new** is _____.
The opposite of **wet** is **dry**.
The opposite of **hello** is _____.

c Find two words in the poem that end in **–y**. Is the sound of **–y** the same or different?

d Circle the words that rhyme in the poem.

6 Act out the Opposites poem.

Think of actions for the opposite words. Say the poem and act it out!

143

8 City places

> 8.6 Sing a Song of People

We are going to...
- read and talk about a poem.

Reading tip

Some words are different in British English and American English. Scan the poem to find the American words written in red. Look at the chart to find the British version of the word.

American English	British English
sidewalk	pavement
subway	underground train
stores	shops
elevators	lifts

1 Listen and read.

This poem was written by an American writer, Lois Lenski.

Sing a Song of People

Sing a song of people
Walking fast or slow;
People in the city,
Up and down they go.

People on the **sidewalk**,
People on the bus;
People passing, passing,
In back and front of us.

8.6 Read and respond

People on the **subway**
Underneath the ground;
People riding taxis
Round and round and round.

People with their hats on,
Going in the doors;
People with umbrellas
When it rains and pours.

People in tall buildings
And in **stores** below;
Riding **elevators**
Up and down they go.

8 City places

People walking singly,
People in a crowd;
People saying nothing,
People talking loud.

People laughing, smiling,
Grumpy people too;
People who just hurry
And never look at you!

Sing a song of people
Who like to come and go;
Sing of city people
You see but never know!

2   Picture search

In the first picture, can you find people on the bus?

In the second picture, can you find:
- people on the subway?
- people with umbrellas?

In the third picture, can you find people in stores?

In the fourth picture, can you find:
- people laughing and smiling?
- grumpy people?

8.6 Read and respond

3 Where is the goose?

The goose is in every picture.
Find him and say where he is.

"Where am I?"

4 Values: We like different things – and that's great!

Some people like living in a big city.

Some people like living in a small town or village.

Some people like living on a farm.

Where do you like living? Ask your friends where they like living.

5 Write a sentence that says where you like living.

Then write some sentences that say **why** you like living there.

Draw a picture.

Share your work with a friend.
Do you like the same things or different things?

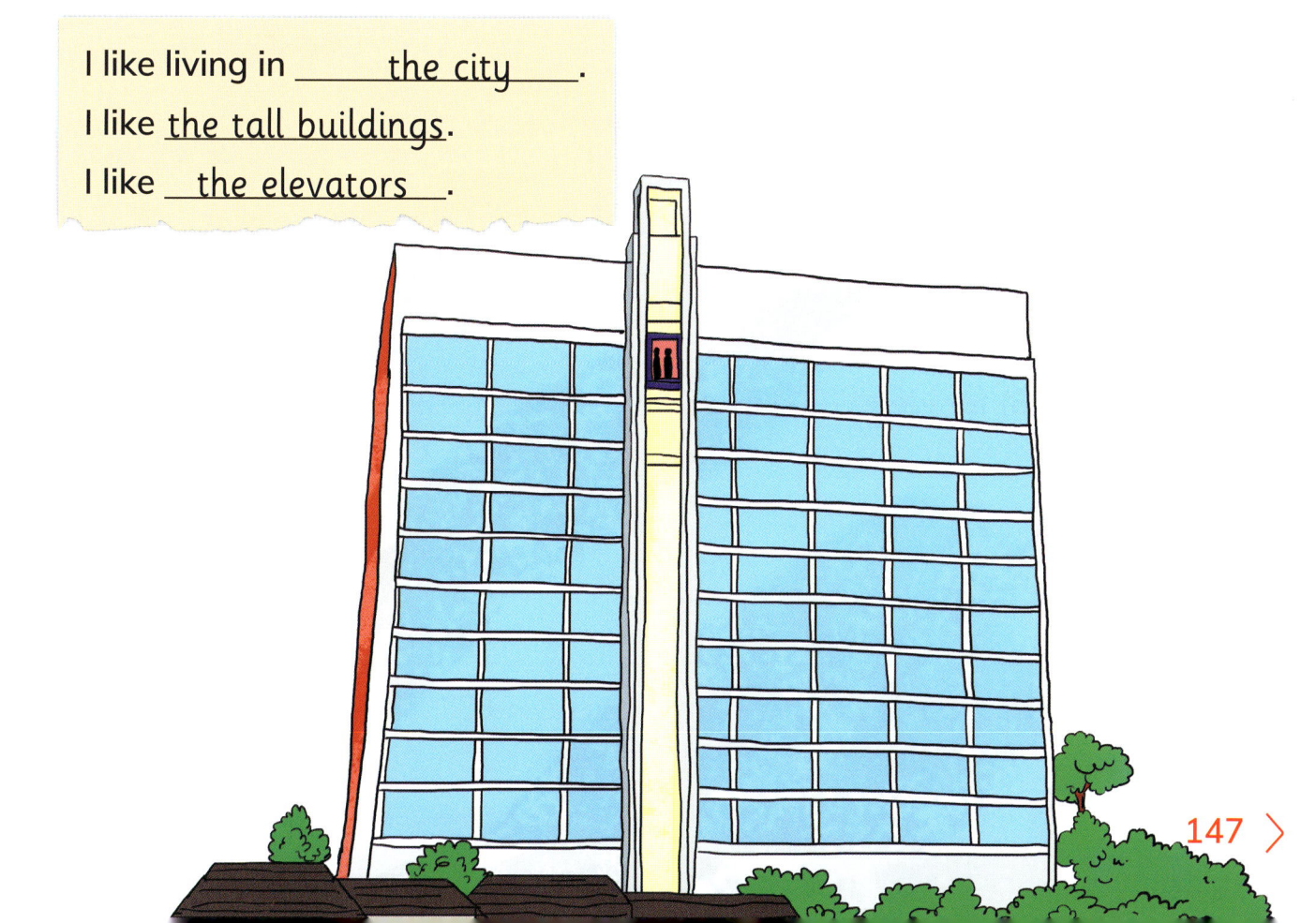

I like living in _____the city_____.
I like the tall buildings.
I like ___the elevators___.

8 City places

> 8.7 Project challenge

Work with a partner or in a group to make the project.
Then share the project with your class.

Project A: Write a poem

Write a poem about your town. Think of things you can see, hear, and smell. Draw a picture.

My town

I can see _____.   I can hear _____.
I can see _____.   I can smell _____.
I can see _____.   My town is _____.

Choose an ending for the last line of your poem:

a busy place   a happy place
a noisy place   a quiet place

Project B: Draw a city map

Make a map of a city, town or village.
Write words on your map.

Look at the Picture dictionary (page 175) for ideas.

8.7 Project challenge

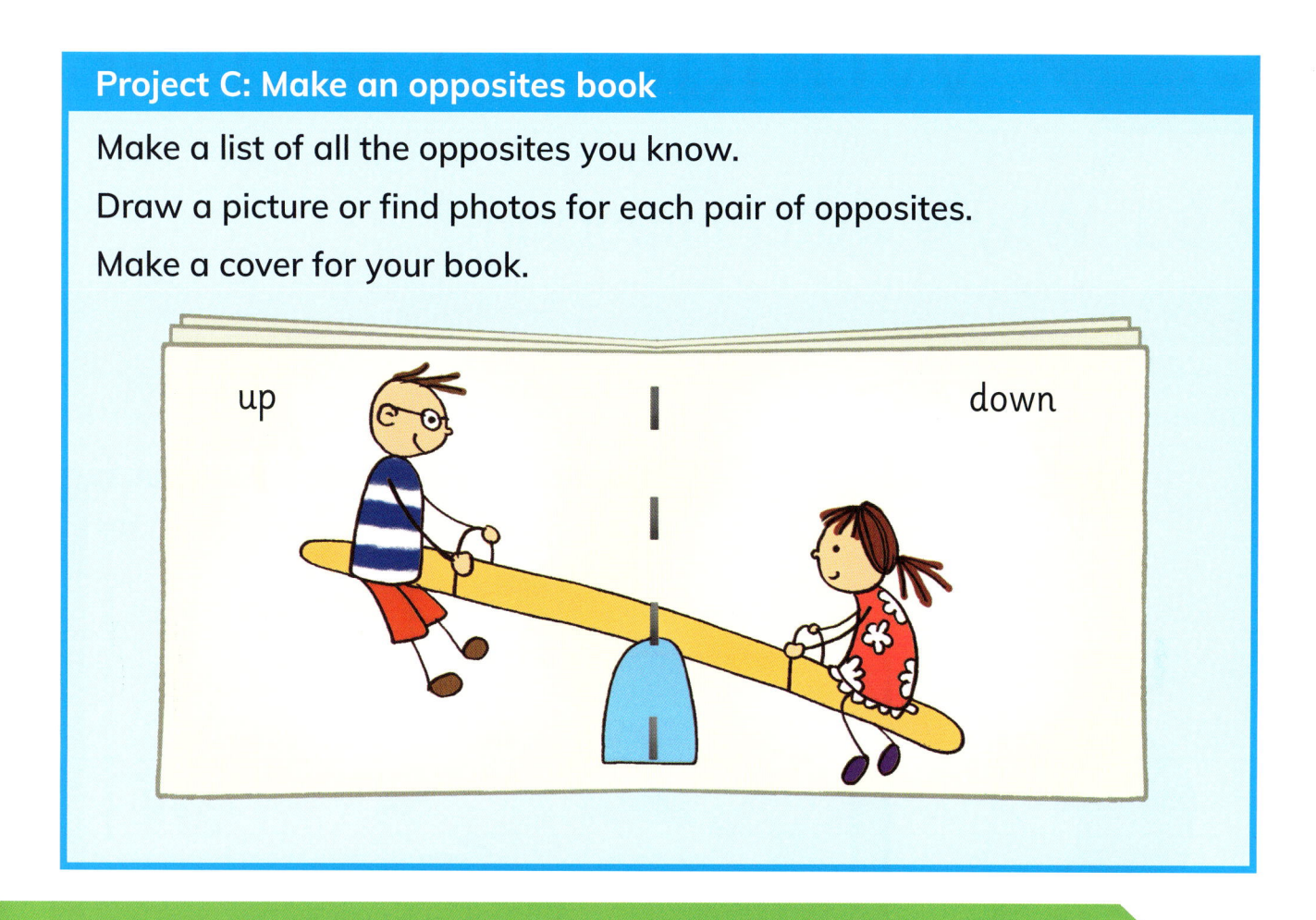

Project C: Make an opposites book

Make a list of all the opposites you know.

Draw a picture or find photos for each pair of opposites.

Make a cover for your book.

up   down

What would you like to do for your next end-of-unit project?

Look what I can do!

I can talk and read about things in a city.

I can describe and ask questions using **this**, **that**, and **these**.

I can read and write words that end in **–y**.

I can name opposites.

I can read and talk about a poem.

9　Wonderful water

> ## 9.1 Why is water important?

We are going to...
- talk about the weather.

Getting started
Why is water important?
Look at the picture for some ideas.

🎧 **1** **What can you see?**

It's a rainy day. The teacher and a girl are looking out of the window.

Listen and point to the things they talk about.

Today is Monday.
It is windy and rainy.

150

9.1 Think about it

2 Listen, point and say.

cloudy windy rainy sunny hot cold

3 Listen and write the letters.

What word do they spell?

4 What's the weather like?

Look at the picture and sentence. What word is missing?

It is hot and _____.

It is snowy and _____.

5 Read and listen.

Put the stickers on as you say the poem.
How can you have fun on a rainy day?

Today it is [rainy].

We can't see the sun.

It's [cloudy] and [windy].

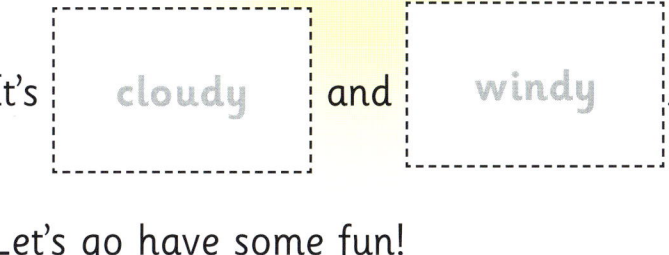

Let's go have some fun!

151

9 Wonderful water

> 9.2 Day by day

We are going to...
- talk about things we do every day.

1 Listen and act.

A girl and her mother are talking.

Listen, then act out the conversation with your partner.

boots    raincoat    umbrella

Don't forget your boots!

Yes, Mum!

2 Read, listen and join in!

Rain on the green grass.
Rain on the tree
Rain on the houses
But not on me!

9.2 Let's explore

3 **Listen to the chant, 'Days of the week'.**

Join in and act out the words.

Monday   Tuesday   Wednesday   Thursday   Friday   Saturday   Sunday

Ask and answer questions with your partner.

What do you do on Tuesday?

On Tuesday, I sing a song

4 **Finish the sentences.**

morning   afternoon   night

What do you do **in the morning**?
What do you do **in the afternoon**?
What do you do **at night**?

Finish the sentences. Look at the pictures for ideas.

a   In the morning, I _____ and _____.

b   In the afternoon, I _____ and _____.

c   At night, I _____ and _____.

do maths at school   eat dinner   get dressed   go to sleep   play with my friends   wake up

5 **Put stickers in your Picture dictionary: eat, play, sleep, wake up.**

On which page do the stickers belong? Find the correct page.

153

9 Wonderful water

> 9.3 Facts about water

We are going to...
- say why plants, animals and people need water.

Reading tip

Before you read, think about what you know.
What do plants need to live and grow?
What do animals need to live and grow?

1 Listen and read.

We all need water

All living things need water.

Plants need water to grow.

Animals need water to drink.

People need water to drink too.

Water comes from rain and snow.

When there is no rain, the land becomes dry and brown.

When rain comes, the land becomes green again.

Plants can grow again.

Animals and people have water to drink again.

All living things need water.

2   Animals that live in water.

Which of these animals live in water? Make a list with your class.

frog   crocodile   hen   turtle   fish   elephant   whale

What other animals live in water?

Look up the English words for the animals in a dictionary.

3   Write about it.

Write about animals that live in water.

Choose three animals.
Fill in the missing words.

Draw a picture.

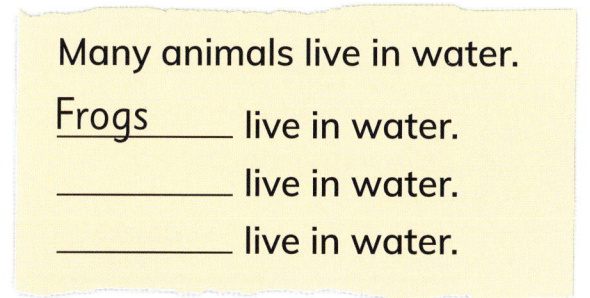

> Many animals live in water.
>
> <u>Frogs</u> live in water.
>
> _____ live in water.
>
> _____ live in water.

Key word

look up

4   We need water.

We need water to make soup.    We need water to wash our hands.

Working in pairs, look at the pictures and read the sentences.

Think of other things we do with water.

We need water to _____.

155

9 Wonderful water

> 9.4 Things that float

We are going to...
- do experiments with things that float and don't float.

1 Does it float?

Some things float. Some things don't.

Look at the picture.

a   Does the apple float?
b   Does the paper clip float?
c   Does the paper boat float?
d   Does the pear float?

Does it float?	
Yes, it does.	No, it doesn't
 🍎	 📎

Say the sentences. Fill in the missing words.

a   The _____ floats.
b   The _____ doesn't float.
c   The paper boat _____.
d   The pear _____ _____.

Language detective

What word joins with **does** to make **doesn't**?

does + _____ = **doesn't**

2 Experiment: Let's find out!

You need:

pencil   paper   elastic band   ruler   leaf   paper clip

First ask your partner,
Does a pencil float? What do you think?

Work in pairs.

Put each thing in a bowl of water.
Record your answer on a chart.

No, I don't think so.

Yes, I think so.

9.4 Use of English

3 **Listen to the song.**

Look at the picture and words.

Sing the song and do the actions.

Row, row, row your boat

Row, row, row your boat,
Gently down the stream.
Merrily, merrily, merrily, merrily,
Life is but a dream.

Row, row, row your boat,
Gently down the stream.
If you see a crocodile,
Don't forget to scream!

Row, row, row your boat,
Gently down the river.
If you see a polar bear,
Don't forget to shiver!

Row, row, row your boat,
Gently in the bath.
If you see a spider,
Don't forget to laugh!

9 Wonderful water

9.5 Long a spellings ai and ay

We are going to...

- read and write words with the long a spellings ai and ay.

1 Listen and read.

Read and listen to the poem. Join in.
Look at the letters ai and ay in the words.
What sound do they make?
Find all the words with this sound.

> Rain, rain, go away.
> Come again some other day.
> All the children want to play.

2 Mystery word

Look at the sentences. Some long a sounds are missing.
Can you guess the missing words?
Write the words:

- Write ai in the middle of a word.
- Write ay at the end of a word.

a It's a r _ _ ny d _ _ .

b Let's p _ _ nt a sn _ _ l.

c Let's pl _ _ with the tr _ _ n.

9.5 Letters and sounds

3 **Read and listen.**

Listen again. Write the words with the long **a** sound.

Please stay and play

It's a rainy day. Little Snail is playing with the frogs and the ducks.

'Goodbye, Little Snail,' the little frogs say.
'Wait, wait! Don't go. Please stay and play.'
'Sorry, Little Snail. We need to go away.'

'Goodbye, Little Snail,' the white ducks say.
'Wait, wait! Don't go. Please stay and play.'
'Sorry, Little Snail. We need to go away.'

'Hello, Little Snail,' the big snails say.
'Hello, big snails! Please stay and play.'
'Sure, Little Snail. We can play all day.'
'Hooray!'

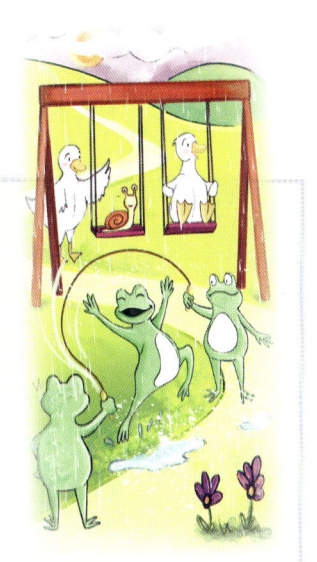

4 **Act it out.**

Who are the characters in the story?
Make a list. Act out the story.

9 Wonderful water

9.6 The Song of the Toad

We are going to...
- read, discuss and act out a folktale.

The Song of the Toad characters

Toad   Rooster   Tiger   Bees

Green Guards   Emperor   Purple Guards

Reading tip

What is a folktale?

A folktale is a story that has been told for many years.

Some folktales answer questions in an interesting, **make-believe** way.

This folktale from Vietnam gives an imaginative answer to the question, 'Why do toads croak before it rains?'

🎧 111 **1 Listen and read.**

The Song of the Toad

The mud is dry.
There is no food to eat.
We need water.

The river is dry.
There is no water to drink.
We need water.

The flowers are dry.
We need flowers to live.
We need water.

Let's go to the Emperor in the castle.
Let's ask the Emperor for rain.

9.6 Read and respond

- Hello. I need to see the Emperor.

- No! You're a toad. A toad can't see the Emperor. Go away.

- Come, Bees! Come, Rooster! Make the Guards go away.

- Buzz, buzz.

- Cock-a-doodle-doo.

- Help! Help!

- Hello, Emperor. I need to talk to you.

- What? Green Guards, come. There's a toad on my lap!

- Come, Tiger! Make the Guards go away.

- ROAR!

- Help! Help!

161

9 Wonderful water

Emperor, the earth is dry. The plants and animals need water. Please send us rain.

OK, I can do that. I can send you rain.

It's raining!

Hooray for the rain!

Thank you, Emperor. The next time we need rain, I will come again.

No, no! Don't come back.

Please don't come back!

Toad, you can sing when you need rain. When I hear your song, I will send the rain.

Thank you, Emperor.

So now, when farmers hear the song of the toad, they are happy.

They know that rain will come soon.

9.6 Read and respond

2 Real or make-believe?

In a folktale, some things are **real**. Many things are **make-believe**.

Which things in *The Song of the Toad* are **real**?
Which things are **make-believe**?

a	Toads sometimes croak before it rains.	real	make-believe
b	Toads can talk to emperors.	real	make-believe
c	Animals need water to live.	real	make-believe
d	Without rain, the earth is dry.	real	make-believe
e	An emperor can make it rain.	real	make-believe

3 Act it out.

Make puppets for the animal characters.

Make hats for the Emperor and the Guards. Act out the play!

4 Values: Water is precious.

Animals, plants and people need water to live and grow.
It is important that we don't waste water.

Talk about the ways that you can save water.
The pictures below will give you some ideas.

5 Writing: My favourite part of the story

Draw a picture of your favourite part of *The Song of the Toad*.

Add a speech bubble.

Write what the character is saying.

9 Wonderful water

> 9.7 Project challenge

Work with a partner or in a group to make the project.

Then share the project with your class.

Project A: Do a weather survey

Make a survey chart. Ask 10 children:

What kind of weather do you like best?						
😓	🧣	🪁	☀️	☁️	☔	❄️
✓		✓✓	✓✓✓✓		✓	✓✓

When your survey is finished, talk about your chart.
- Which weather do most children like best?
- Which weather do fewest children like best?

Project B: Write a book or make a slideshow about water

Write a book or make a slideshow with your group called 'We All Need Water'.

Think about people, animals and plants. Why do we all need water?

Write a sentence on each page.

Draw pictures or use photos from the computer.

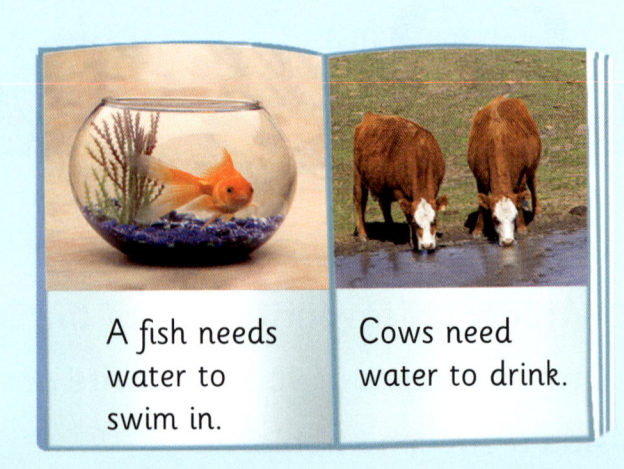

A fish needs water to swim in.

Cows need water to drink.

9.7 Project challenge

Project C: Do an experiment: Does your boat float?

Make a boat from paper and tape.

Put **2** coins in your boat.
Put **5** coins in your boat.
Put **10** coins in your boat.

Does your boat float?

Record the information in a table, like this.

	Does your boat float?	
	Yes, it does.	No, it doesn't.
with 0 coins?	✔	
with 2 coins?	✔	
with 5 coins?		
with 10 coins?		

Make a boat from foil, wood or plastic.
Try the same experiment.

Which boat can carry the most coins?

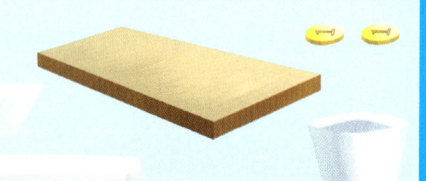

What would you do differently if you did this project again?

Look what I can do!

I can talk about the weather.

I can talk about things we do every day.

I can say why plants, animals, and people need water.

I can do experiments with things that float and don't float.

I can read and write words with the long **a** spellings **ai** and **ay**.

I can read, discuss and act out a play.

9 Units 7–9: Review

Check your progress
City fun

You need:
- 2 to 3 players
- a different game marker for each player
- number cards.

Directions

Step 1. Take a number card.

Step 2. Count and move your game marker on the game track. Then do one of these things:
- Read the **sentences**. Say the missing word. Go to the matching picture.
- Look at the picture. Say the word.
- Read and answer the **question** or do the **action**.

Step 3. The first player to get HOME is the winner!

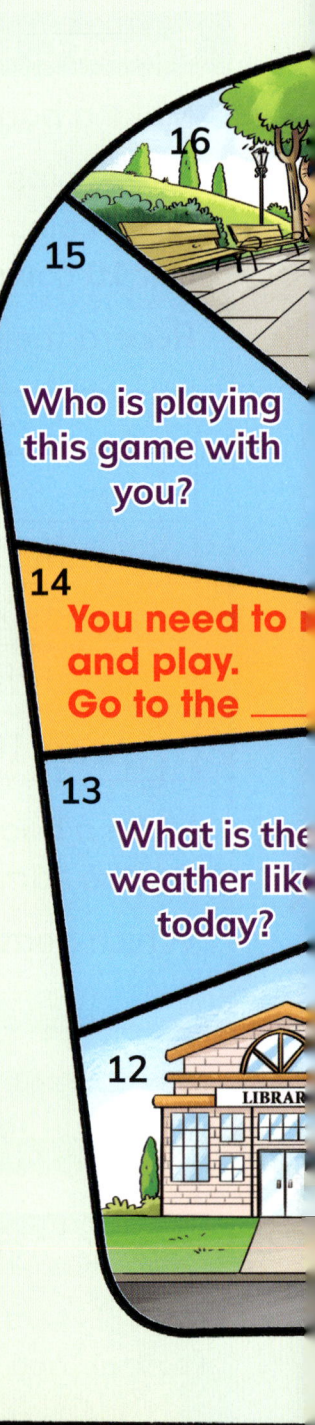

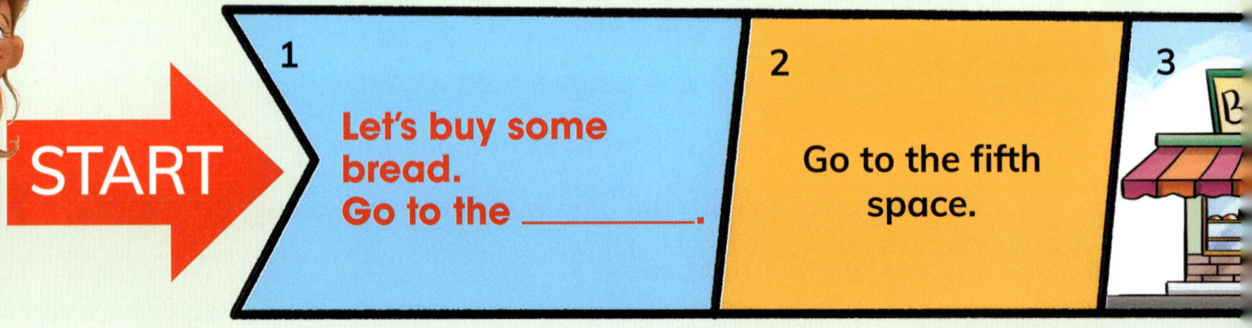

16

15 Who is playing this game with you?

14 You need to and play. Go to the ____

13 What is the weather like today?

12 LIBRARY

START

1 Let's buy some bread. Go to the _____.

2 Go to the fifth space.

3

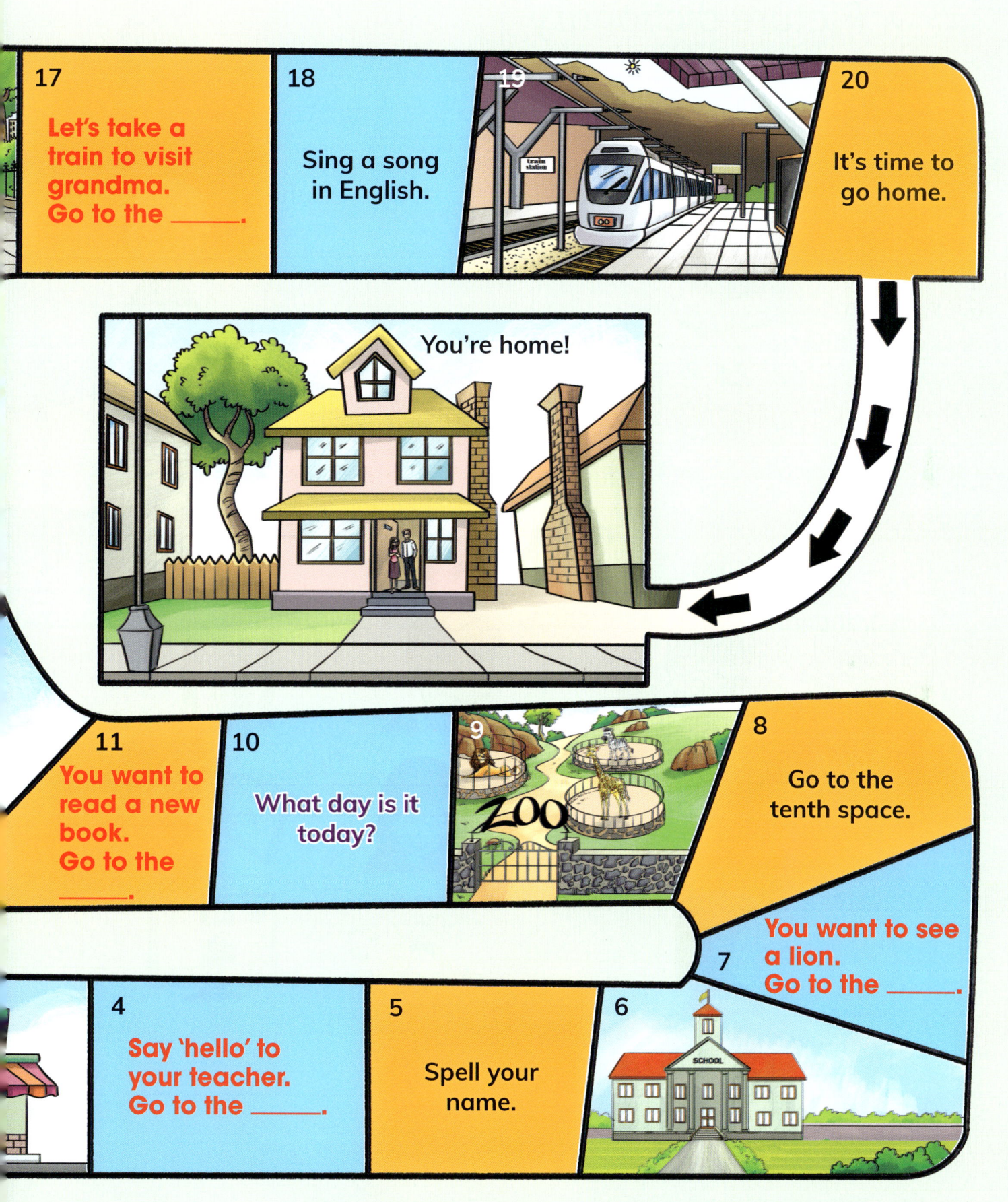

Check your progress: City fun

17 Let's take a train to visit grandma. Go to the _____.

18 Sing a song in English.

19

20 It's time to go home.

You're home!

11 You want to read a new book. Go to the _____.

10 What day is it today?

9

8 Go to the tenth space.

7 You want to see a lion. Go to the _____.

4 Say 'hello' to your teacher. Go to the _____.

5 Spell your name.

6

167

› Picture dictionary

1 Home and family

baby		bed		brother	
ceiling		children		dad/father	
door		family		floor	
grandma		grandpa		grown-ups	
house		mum/mother		rug	
sister		teddy bear		TV	
window					

2 School

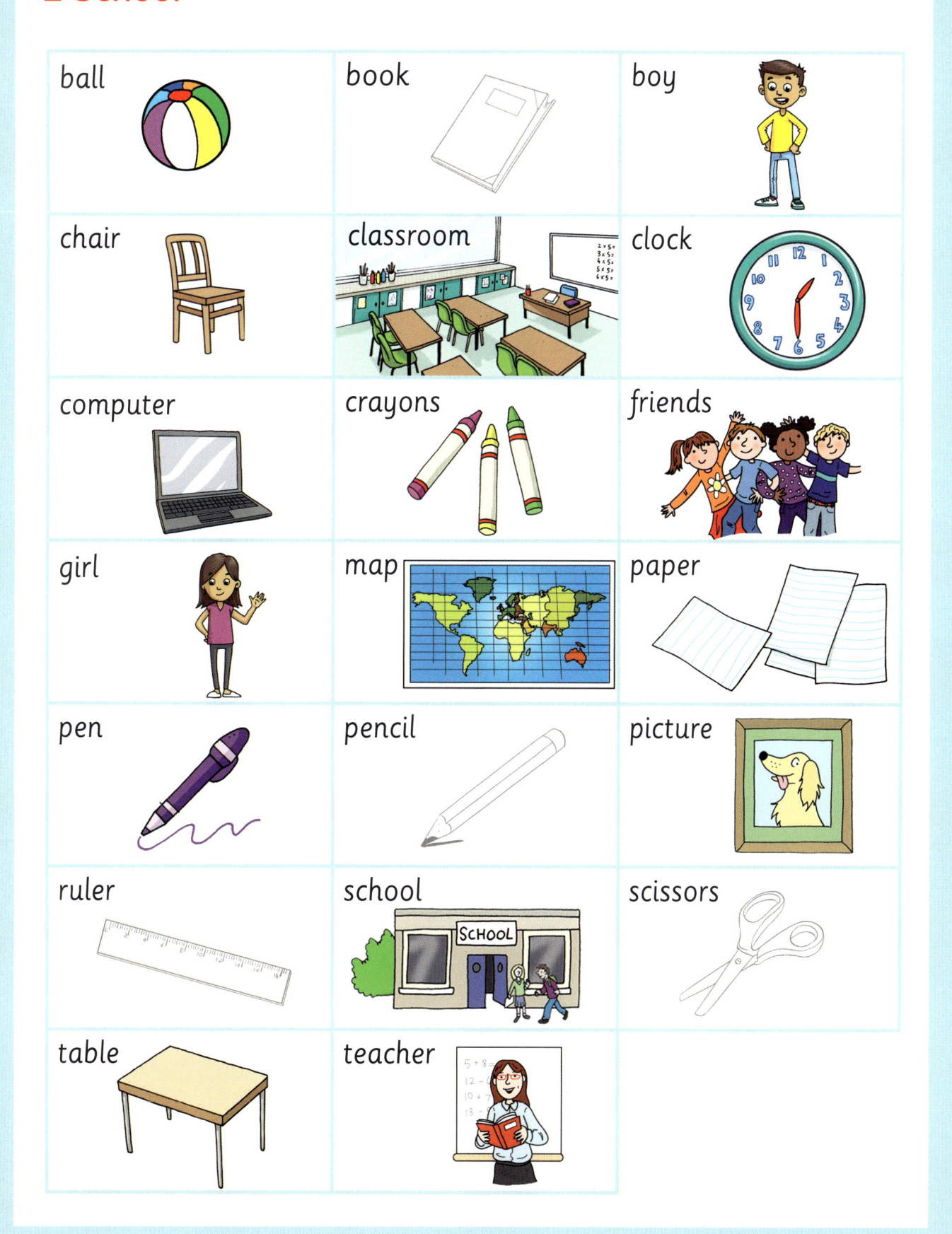

ball	book	boy
chair	classroom	clock
computer	crayons	friends
girl	map	paper
pen	pencil	picture
ruler	school	scissors
table	teacher	

169

3 The body and clothes

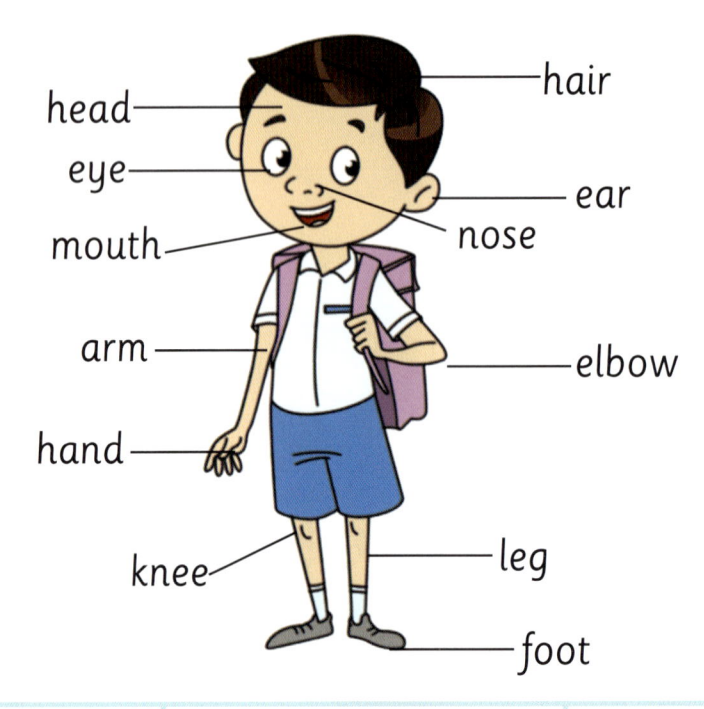

- head
- hair
- eye
- ear
- mouth
- nose
- arm
- elbow
- hand
- knee
- leg
- foot

boots	dress	glasses
hat	jacket	raincoat
shirt	shoes	skirt
trousers		

4 Food

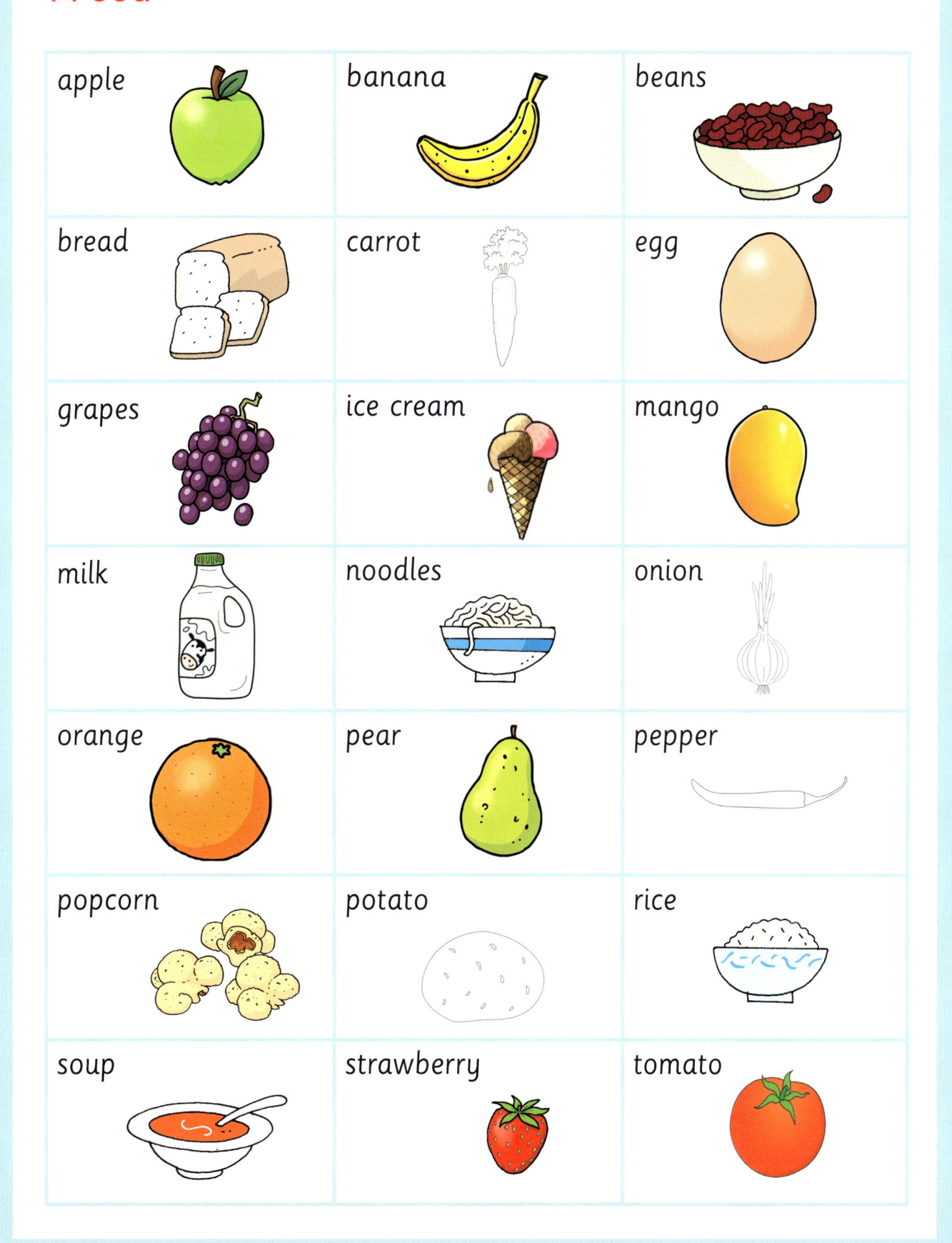

apple	banana	beans
bread	carrot	egg
grapes	ice cream	mango
milk	noodles	onion
orange	pear	pepper
popcorn	potato	rice
soup	strawberry	tomato

5 Actions

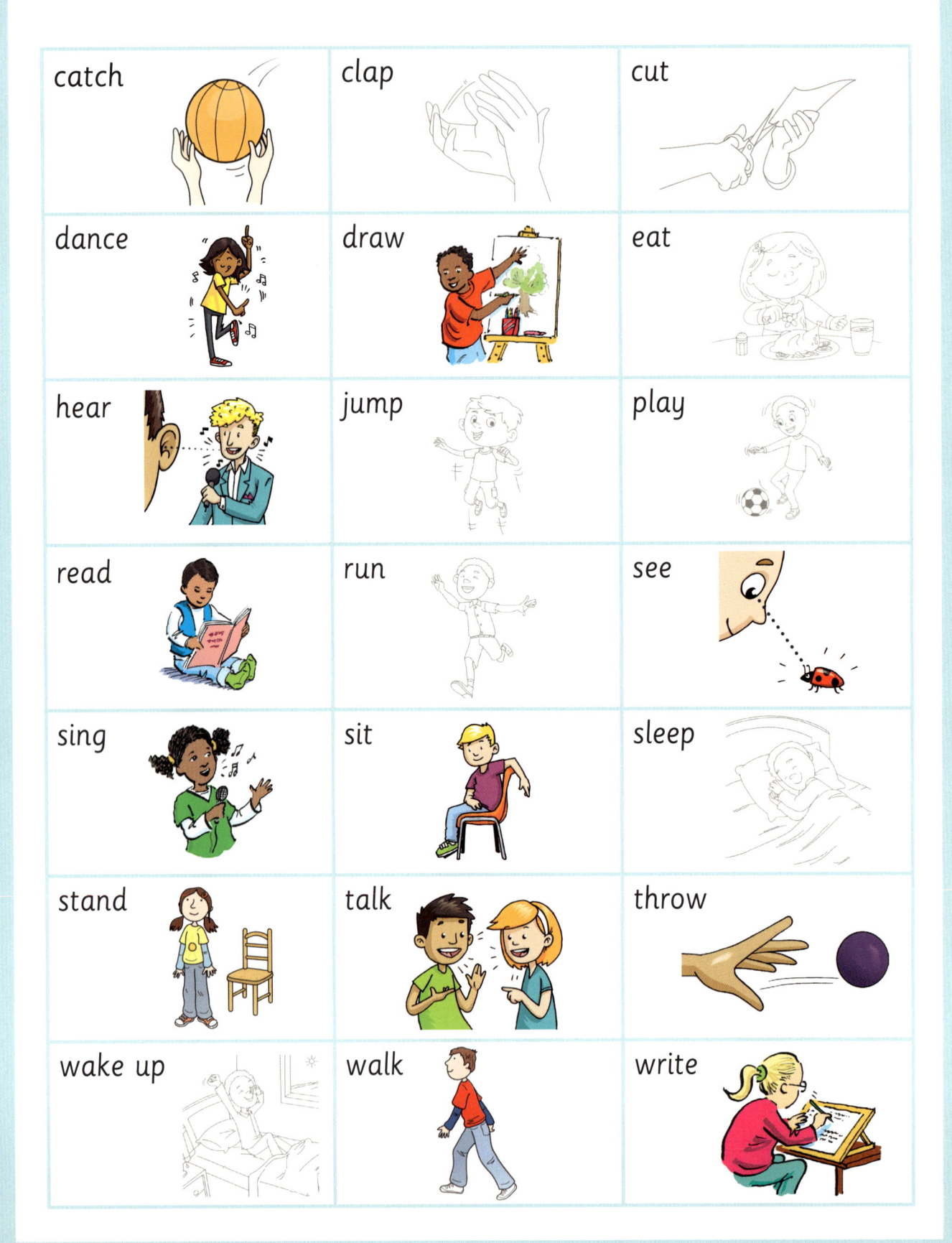

catch	clap	cut
dance	draw	eat
hear	jump	play
read	run	see
sing	sit	sleep
stand	talk	throw
wake up	walk	write

6 Animals

bee	bird	cat
chick	cow	deer
dog	duck	elephant
fish	fox	frog
goat	hen	horse
rabbit	rooster	sheep
snail	tiger	turtle

7 Nature and weather

cloud	day	flower
garden	grass	lake
leaf	log	mountain
night	pond	rain
river	rock	seed
sky	snow	stick
sun	tree	water

8 The city (and transport)

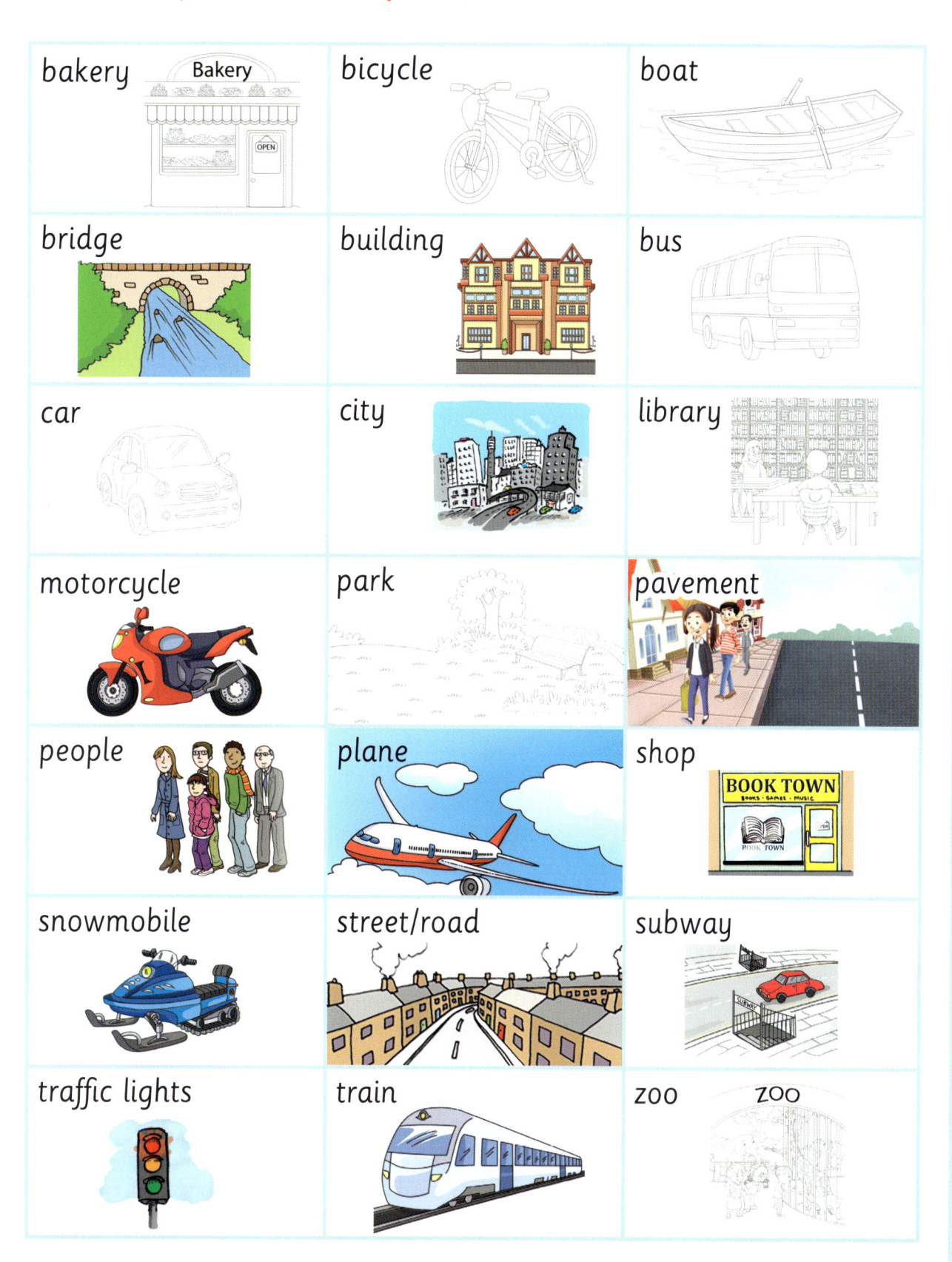

bakery	bicycle	boat
bridge	building	bus
car	city	library
motorcycle	park	pavement
people	plane	shop
snowmobile	street/road	subway
traffic lights	train	zoo

Acknowledgements

The authors and publishers acknowledge the following sources of copyright material and are grateful for the permissions granted. While every effort has been made, it has not always been possible to identify the sources of all the material used, or to trace all copyright holders. If any omissions are brought to our notice, we will be happy to include the appropriate acknowledgements on reprinting. The authors and publishers would like to thank the following for reviewing Stage 1: Jordan Olson, Judy Casiechetty, Nidhi Chopra.

'Breakfast Bowl' song written by Mark Baldwin, used by kind permission.

'Sing a Song of People' by Lois Lenski Covey Foundation Inc., reprinted by permission of SLL/Sterling Lord Literistic, Inc. Copyright by Lois Lenski.

Other songs and music throughout are reproduced from *Primary Music Box* © Cambridge University Press

Thanks to the following for permission to reproduce images:
Cover by Omar Aranda (Beehive Illustration); *Inside* Unit 0 p12 MichaelH/GI; Herjua/GI; Sleepyz/GI; Francisgonsa/GI; filo/GI; briang/GI; Unit 1 clubfoto/GI; Gallo Images/GI; Chris Stowers/Panos Pictures; Wavebreakmedia/GI; Cavan Images/GI; AAREF WATAD/GI; Tom Grill/GI; BIJU BORO/GI; Stuart Fox/GI; JW LTD/GI Stockbyte/GI; Hill Street Studios/GI; Chee Siong Teh/GI; MoMoProductions/GI; Unit 2 kiankhoon/GI; Yevgen Romanenko/GI; ValentynVolkov/GI; Unit 3 stevezmina1/GI; Sorapong Chaipanya/EyeEm/GI; simmosimosa/GI; Photoevent/GI; Mimi Haddon/GI; Unit 4 iStock; Natalie_/GI; Unit 5 Photo and Co/GI; Michael Fairchild/GI; Fei Yang/GI; Lesley Middlemiss Lister/GI; Mordolff/GI; GlobalP/GI; Nik_Merkulov/GI; Skodonnell/GI; Elles Rijsdijk/GI; Ryan McVay/GI; MahirAtes/GI; Aluxum/GI; Redmal/GI; KentWeakley/GI; Stepbar/GI; Carlos Sussmann/GI; NREY/GI; Ljupco/GI; Ljupco/GI; Aluxum/GI; Unit 6 kool99/GI; artpartner-images/GI; Mint Images – Jamel Toppin/GI; Olga Guchek/GI; Hdagli/GI; Vstock LLC/GI; ALEAIMAGE/GI; Turnervisual/GI; undefined undefined/GI; Devonyu/GI; Chictype/GI; ConstantinosZ/GI; Moonisblack/GI; Issauinko/GI Roman Samokhin/GI; DanielMenR/GI; claudiodivizia/GI Kovaleva_Ka/GI; Roman Samokhin/GI; Roman Samokhin/GI; Rawf8/GI; nipastock/GI; Star Tribune/GI; Unit 7 Zoonar GmbH/Alamy Stock Photo; Nick Kee Son/GI; deebrowning/GI; imagenavi/GI; martin-dm/GI; Marilyn Nieves/GI; GordanD/GI; OlgaIngs/GI; Claudiodivizia/GI; Christopher Kontoes/GI; Marcduf/GI; Zero Creatives/GI; Trevor Williams/GI; Monty Rakusen/GI; Dsafanda/GI; Daniel Milchev/GI; gldburger/GI; Vivian Fung/Shutterstock; Unit 8 venakr/GI; Pakin Songmor/GI; Martin Wahlborg/GI; Muhamad Norsaifudin Sulaiman/GI; Curtoicurto/GI; Alexey_Fedoren/GI; Spondylolithesis/GI; Richard Newstead/GI; Tholer/GI; FabrikaCr/GI; EarnestTse/GI; Sasiistock/GI; Venakr/GI; Kemter/GI; Riccardo Lennart Niels Mayer/GI; Iliana Mestari/GI; Tioloco/GI; Stefan Ziese/GI; SDI Productions/GI; Martin-dm/GI; Gizelka/GI; OwenPrice/GI; Peathegee Inc/GI; JethuynhCan/GI; Tang Ming Tung/GI; Unit 9 LeManna/GI; LWA/Dann Tardif/GI evgenyatamanenko/GI; Adam Hester/GI; Dennis K. Johnson/GI; 184127455/GI; Piyaset/GI; RuslanDashinsky/GI; Rattankun Thongbun/GI; Navaswan/GI MidwestWilderness/GI

GI = Getty Images

Development of this publication has made use of the Cambridge English Corpus (CEC). The CEC is a multi-billion word computer database of contemporary spoken and written English. It includes British English, American English and other varieties of English. It also includes the Cambridge Learner Corpus, developed in collaboration with Cambridge Assessment English. Cambridge University Press has built up the CEC to provide evidence about language use that helps to produce better language teaching materials.

Stickers for Starter Unit page 15

Stickers for Unit 1 page 19

table  | chairs 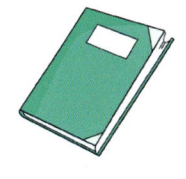 | book  | crayons

Stickers for Unit 2 page 35

family  | father  | mother  | brother

Stickers for Unit 3 page 51

Bounce 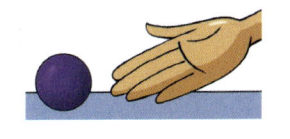 | Roll  | throw  | Catch

Stickers for Unit 4 page 69

glasses  | skirt  | shirt

Stickers for Unit 5 page 85

tractor 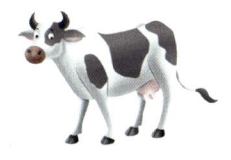　　cow 　　sheep 　　hens

Stickers for Unit 6 page 101

see 　　hear 　　smell 　　taste

Stickers for Unit 7 page 119

climb 　　slide 　　float 　　drive

Stickers for Unit 8 page 135

Roads 　　pavements 　　shops 　　traffic

Stickers for Unit 9 page 151

rainy 　　cloudy 　　windy

Stickers for Picture dictionary Starter Unit page 15

book

pencil

ruler

scissors

Stickers for Picture dictionary Unit 1 page 23

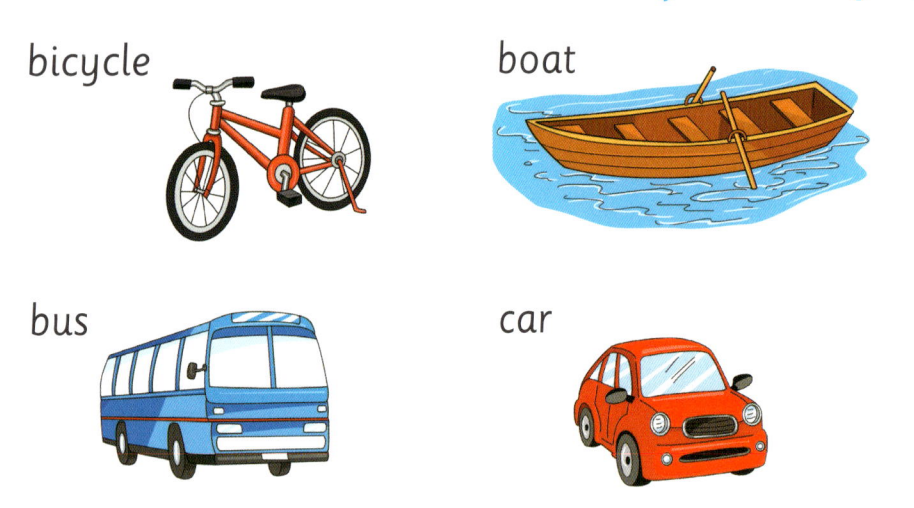

bicycle

boat

bus

car

Stickers for Picture dictionary Unit 2 page 38

house

door

window

bed

Stickers for Picture dictionary Unit 3 page 59

clap

cut

jump

run

Stickers for Picture dictionary Unit 4 page 81

shoes

boots

jacket

hat

Stickers for Picture dictionary Unit 5 page 90

carrot

pepper

onion

potato

Stickers for Picture dictionary Unit 9 page 153

eat

play

sleep

wake up